Let's Party

COOKBOOK

Credits

Great American Opportunities, Inc.
Favorite Recipes® Press

President:
Thomas F. McDow III
Vice President:
Dave Kempf
Managing Editor:
Mary Cummings
Senior Editors:
Georgia Brazil, Jane Hinshaw, Linda Jones,
Charlene Sproles, Debbie Van Mol, Mary Wilson
Associate Editors:
Lucinda Anderson, Judy Jackson, Carolyn King,
Elizabeth Miller, Judy Van Dyke
Production Designer:
Pam Newsome
Typographers:
Jessie Anglin, Sara Anglin
Production:
John Moulton
Production Assistants:
George McAlister, Karen McClain

This cookbook is a collection of our favorite recipes,
which are not necessarily original recipes.

Published by:
Favorite Recipes® Press, a division of
Great American Opportunities, Inc.
P.O. Box 305142
Nashville, Tennessee 37230
1-800-358-0560

Manufactured in the United States of America
First Printing: 1995   50,000 copies

Recipes for cover photograph are not available.

Contents

Let's Party

Affairs to Remember

Of all the many parties we attend, undoubtedly those that tend to stand out most in our memories are theme parties. Whether they are wild and woolly or subdued and elegant, theme parties give the hostess a wonderful opportunity to really stretch creatively, tying food, decoration, costume, invitations, music, and table settings all together in one great big, beautiful package.

These may be the most "fun" parties of all, where we let our hair down, laugh a little at ourselves, and amuse each other with wit and good humor. A party theme can come from almost anywhere—the sky's the limit.

Tax-time blues got you and your friends down? Why not cheer up with a Tay Payer's Bawl on April 15? Or take advantage of the current exercise craze with a Carbo-Loading Pasta Party.

Current events are often a source of themes, like an Inaugural Gala, where guests come dressed as presidents and first ladies, items from White House menus are served, and prizes are given for winners of presidential trivia games. On the zanier side of things, give a couch potato party, where all menu items are based on potatoes, or a wonderfully tacky party, where you can surrender to that urge to serve up heaps of moon pies, Spam, and peanut butter crackers. Just let your imagination lead you where it will. The idea is to have fun!

Seasonal Samplers

Whether you celebrate Christmas under the palms, or define summer as two months of warmth sandwiched between snowstorms, you undoubtedly associate certain special kinds of entertaining with each season. Seasonal changes present us with wonderful opportunities for party giving, and wise hosts know that one of the secrets of successful entertaining is taking advantage of these.

Fall parties can take on a harvest theme, celebrate the glorious golds, reds, and russets of the changing season. With events from football games to Halloween and Thanksgiving, autumn is a great season for entertaining.

In winter, major holidays take the spotlight. Our suggestions for Christmas include classic dinners as well as lighthearted ideas such as a Christmas tree caper. For New Year's, why not try a daytime open house in lieu of the standby New Year's Eve party? Or warm up informally with a snowy chili supper.

In spring, graduations, weddings, and other special days fill our social calendars, along with Easter and Mother's Day. It is also the time when gardens provide the stuff great menus are made of.

Last, but in no way least, on our entertaining calendar is summer, the time of the year when easy, breezy parties come into their own and make the most of the good times and good food of the season.

Occasional Occasions

Most of the time, we think of social events as Big Occasions, parties that mark particularly important happenings in our lives. These are wonderful gatherings, often characterized by elaborate menus and extensive preparation. But why wait for a "capital O" occasion to roll around for a party? Even the most commonplace event can inspire a grand celebration.

The approach of *any* weekend is cause for festivities. You might host a tantalizing dessert buffet in honor of the end of winter doldrums or a football widow's brunch when the season comes.

Whatever your preferences and style of entertaining, use these suggestions to brighten up your next event. Remember, there is a party out there just waiting to happen!

Grazing

Appetizers

Almond-Bacon-Cheese Crostini

1 French baguette
2 slices bacon, crisp-fried, crumbled
1 cup (113 g) shredded Monterey Jack cheese
1/3 cup (74 g) mayonnaise or mayonnaise-type salad dressing

1/4 cup (24 g) toasted sliced almonds
1 tablespoon (6.3 g) chopped green onions
1/4 teaspoon (1.4 g) salt

Slice baguette into 36 pieces. Place cut side down on foil-lined baking sheet. Bake at 400° F (204° C) for 5 minutes or until lightly browned. Mix bacon, cheese, mayonnaise, almonds, green onions and salt in bowl. Spread over bread slices. Bake for 5 minutes or until cheese is melted. Garnish with toasted sliced almonds. Yield: 36 servings.

Dodie Dorton, Manchester High School, Manchester, OH

Broccoli Cheese Pinwheels

2¹/₃ cups (292 g) **self-rising flour**
¹/₄ teaspoon (.8 g) **baking soda**
1 teaspoon (3.1 g) **sesame or poppy seeds**
¹/₃ cup (68 g) **shortening**
1 cup (245 g) **buttermilk**

1 (10-ounce) (284-g) **package chopped broccoli, cooked, drained**
1 cup (113 g) **shredded Cheddar cheese**

Mix flour, baking soda and sesame seeds in bowl. Cut in shortening until crumbly. Stir in buttermilk. Knead lightly on floured board. Roll ¹/₄ inch (.75 cm) thick. Spread broccoli and cheese over dough. Roll up as for jelly roll; cut ¹/₂ inch (1.5 cm) thick and seal edges. Place on baking sheet. Bake at 400° F (204° C) for 10 to 12 minutes or until cheese is melted.
Yield: 12 servings.

Deborah Carter, Floyd County High School, Floyd, VA

Cheese Wafers

1 cup (227 g) **margarine**
2 cups (250 g) **flour**
8 ounces (227 g) **sharp Cheddar cheese, shredded**

1 teaspoon (1.8 g) **cayenne**
¹/₂ teaspoon (2.8 g) **salt**
2 cups (28 g) **puffed rice**

Cut margarine into flour in bowl. Add cheese, pepper and salt; mix well. Stir in cereal. Drop by spoonfuls onto ungreased baking sheet. Flatten with spoon. Bake at 350° F (177° C) for 15 minutes; do not overbrown.
Yield: 24 servings.

Donna McKethan, Bosqueville High School, Waco, TX

A Party Hint

A single rule of thumb allows two to four appetizers per person.

Mexican Fudge

2 cups (226 g) **shredded
Cheddar or Colby cheese
2 cups** (226 g) **Monterey Jack
cheese**

¹/₂ cup (64 g) **hot taco sauce
3 eggs**

Mix cheeses in bowl. Pat ¹/₂ of the mixture into 8x8-inch (20x20-cm) baking pan. Beat taco sauce with eggs in bowl. Pour into pan. Add remaining cheese mixture. Bake at 350° F (177° C) for 30 minutes. Cut into squares. Serve on crackers or tortilla chips. Yield: 16 servings.

*Charlotte Guelbert
El Dorado Springs High School, El Dorado Springs, MO*

Mozzarella and Bacon Bread

**1 loaf French bread, sliced
3 cups** (339 g) **shredded
mozzarella cheese
¹/₂ pound** (227 g) **bacon, cut into
small pieces**

¹/₂ cup (80 g) **finely chopped
onion
¹/₂ cup** (114 g) **melted margarine
¹/₃ cup** (83 g) **mustard**

Spray a foil-lined baking sheet with nonstick cooking spray. Place bread on baking sheet. Top with cheese, bacon and onion. Mix margarine with mustard in bowl. Pour over bread. Bake at 350° F (177° C) for 30 minutes or until bacon is browned and crisp. Yield: 10 to 12 servings.

Vickie Bruce, Lake Hamilton Junior High School, Pearcy, AR

A Party Hint

To avoid having to repeat what is being served, write names of appetizers on theme-related place cards and place them next to the appetizers. This also prevents waste—guests won't take appetizers they don't like.

Parmesan and Bacon Crackers

1 pound (454 g) **bacon**
1 (16-ounce) (454-g) **package**
  Waverly crackers

Grated Parmesan cheese to taste
Garlic salt to taste

Cut each bacon slice into 6 equal pieces. Wrap 1 piece around center of each cracker. Place in jelly roll pan. Sprinkle with cheese and garlic salt. Bake at 200° F (93° C) for 2 hours and 30 minutes. Store in airtight container. Serve at room temperature or reheat. Yield: 40 to 50 servings.

Alissa Regitz, West Millbrook Middle School, Raleigh, NC

Zesty Chicken Puffs

1 cup (237 g) **water**
1/2 cup (114 g) **butter or**
  margarine
1/4 teaspoon (1.4 g) **salt**
1 cup (125 g) **flour**
4 eggs
3 (5-ounce) (142-g) **cans chicken**
  spread

1 tablespoon (3.5 g) **instant**
  minced onion
3 hard-cooked eggs, chopped
2 tablespoons (31 g) **lemon juice**
1/4 cup (58 g) **sour cream with**
  chives

Bring water, butter and salt to a boil in saucepan; remove from heat. Stir in flour all at once; beat well until mixture leaves sides of pan. Cool for 1 minute. Add 4 eggs 1 at a time, beating well after each addition; mixture should be smooth and glossy. Place 1-inch (2.5-cm) mounds 2 inches (5 cm) apart on greased baking sheets. Bake at 450° F (232° C) for 15 minutes. Reduce oven temperature to 350° F (177° C). Bake for 10 minutes or until shells are golden brown and sides are dry and rigid. Combine chicken spread, onion, eggs, lemon juice and sour cream in bowl; mix well. Chill for 15 minutes. Spoon into baked puffs. May freeze puffs after baking. Yield: 48 servings.

Barbara Ward, Dalton High School, Dalton, GA

Foxy Frank Appetizers

1 cup (320 g) apricot preserves
1/2 cup (123 g) tomato sauce
1/3 cup (80 g) white vinegar
1/4 cup (59 g) cooking sherry
2 tablespoons (42 g) honey
1 tablespoon (14 g) salad oil

1/4 teaspoon (.5 g) ground ginger
1 teaspoon (5.5 g) salt
2 tablespoons (36 g) soy sauce
2 pounds (907 g) frankfurters,
    cut into 1-inch (2.5-cm) pieces

Combine all ingredients except frankfurters in skillet; mix well. Stir in frankfurters. Simmer, covered, for 15 to 20 minutes or until heated through. Serve hot on wooden picks. Yield: 60 servings.

Deborah Burmer, Tazewell Middle School, Tazewell, VA

Ham Balls

1 pound (454 g) ground cured
    ham
1 pound (454 g) ground fresh
    ham
1 egg
1 cup (100 g) bread crumbs
1/2 teaspoon (1.1 g) pepper

1/2 cup (122 g) milk
1/2 cup (120 g) vinegar
1/2 cup (119 g) water
1 cup (181 g) packed brown
    sugar
1 teaspoon (5.2 g) mustard

Combine ham, egg, bread crumbs, pepper and milk in bowl; mix well. Shape into walnut-sized balls. Chill for several hours. Place in 9x13-inch (23x33-cm) baking pan. Mix vinegar, water, brown sugar and mustard in bowl. Pour into pan. Bake, covered, at 350° F (177° C) for 40 minutes. Bake, uncovered, for 30 minutes longer. Yield: 24 to 30 servings.

Sue Reynolds, Bartlesville High School, Bartlesville, OK

Ham and Cheese Party Rolls

3 packages party rolls
1 cup (227 g) butter or
  margarine, softened
2 tablespoons (31 g) prepared
  mustard
2 teaspoons (11 g)
  Worcestershire sauce

1 small onion, grated
2 tablespoons (18 g) poppy seeds
1 pound (454 g) baked ham,
  grated or sliced
3/4 pound (340 g) Swiss cheese,
  shredded

Split rolls into 2 layers horizontally. Mix remaining ingredients in bowl. Spread over bottom layer of rolls; replace top layer. Place in baking pan. Bake at 325° F (163 C) for 12 to 15 minutes or until cheese is melted. Serve warm. May microwave 12 rolls at a time on High for 1 to 1 1/2 minutes. Yield: 36 servings.

Sharon Rhudy, Tazewell High School, Tazewell, VA
Carole C. DeArman, Berkner High School, Richardson, TX

Ham Roll-Ups

3 ounces (85 g) cream cheese
  with chives, softened

1 (7-ounce) (198-g) package
  sliced ham or turkey

Spread cream cheese on ham slices. Roll up; secure with wooden picks. Chill until serving time. Cut into 1/2-inch (1.5-cm) pieces. Yield: 50 servings.

Lynn A. Burch, Fannin County High School, Blue Ridge, GA

A Party Hint

When freezing party foods, take special care in packaging. Place in rigid containers so the goodies will not be crushed.

Olive Ham Appetizers

3/4 cup (105 g) **cooked ground ham**
1/2 cup (85 g) **chopped olives**
1 tablespoon (14 g) **sour cream**
1 teaspoon (5.2 g) **mustard**
1 teaspoon (5.7 g) **Worcestershire sauce**

1 recipe (1-crust) **all-ready pie pastry**
1 tablespoon (6.7 g) **caraway seeds**

Mix ham, olives, sour cream, mustard and Worcestershire sauce in bowl. Divide pastry dough into 6 portions. Roll each portion into 3x5-inch (7.5x13-cm) rectangle. Sprinkle 1/2 teaspoon (1.1 g) caraway seeds over each. Spread with olive mixture. Roll up dough, starting at long ends; pinch to seal but do not close ends of rolls. Place on baking sheet. Bake at 450° F (232° C) for 12 minutes. Cut into slices. Yield: 20 servings.

Lisa Krompien and Jane Balgeman
Manhattan High School, Manhattan, MT

Cocktail Meatballs

1 pound (454 g) **ground beef or ground chuck**
1/3 cup (53 g) **minced onion**
1/2 cup (50 g) **dry bread crumbs**
1/4 cup (61 g) **milk**
1 **egg**
1 teaspoon (1.3 g) **parsley**
1/2 teaspoon (2.8 g) **salt**

1/8 teaspoon (.3 g) **pepper**
1/2 teaspoon (2.8 g) **Worcestershire sauce**
1 (12-ounce) (340-g) **bottle chili sauce**
1 (10-ounce) (284-g) **jar grape jelly**

Mix ground beef, onion, bread crumbs, milk, egg, parsley, salt, pepper and Worcestershire sauce in bowl. Shape into 3/4-inch (2.5-cm) balls. Place in baking pan. Bake at 350° F (177° C) for 20 to 25 minutes or until browned. Mix chili sauce with jelly in saucepan. Cook until jelly is melted, stirring constantly. Add meatballs, stirring to coat. Simmer for 5 to 10 minutes or until heated through. May serve in fondue or chafing dish.
Yield: 12 to 15 servings.

Jan Driscoll, Myndersi Academy, Seneca Falls, NY

Black Olive-Stuffed Mushrooms

15 mushrooms
½ cup (50 g) grated Parmesan
  cheese
½ cup (85 g) chopped pitted
  black olives

1 tablespoon (17 g)
  Worcestershire sauce
8 slices bacon, crisp-fried,
  crumbled

Clean mushrooms with damp paper towels; remove and discard stems. Mix cheese, olives and Worcestershire sauce in bowl. Spoon into mushroom caps. Sprinkle with bacon. Place in 9x13-inch (23x33-cm) baking dish. Bake at 350° F (177° C) for 10 to 15 minutes or until lightly browned. Yield: 15 servings.

Mary Jo Holbrook, Westland High School, Galloway, OH

Picante Super Skillet Nachos

1 pound (454 g) ground beef
1 onion, chopped
2 cups (453 g) picante sauce
1 (15-ounce) (425-g) can pinto
  beans, rinsed, drained
1 teaspoon (2.5 g) chili powder
1 tomato, chopped
1 large or 2 small avocados,
  chopped

1½ cups (255 g) sliced black
  olives
1 cup (113 g) shredded Cheddar
  cheese
½ to 1 cup (115 to 230 g) sour
  cream
Tortilla chips to taste

Brown ground beef with onion in 12-inch (30-cm) skillet; drain. Add picante sauce, beans and chili powder. Bring to a boil; reduce heat. Simmer for 5 minutes. Stir in tomato, avocado and olives; remove from heat. Sprinkle with cheese. Stir in sour cream. Place a row of tortilla chips around edge of skillet. Serve with additional tortilla chips and picante sauce. Yield: 6 to 8 servings.

Karen Anderson, Duncanville 9th Grade, Duncanville, TX

Vegetable Nachos

9 (6-inch) (15-cm) **corn tortillas**
1 cup (180 g) **chopped tomato**
¼ cup (25 g) **chopped green bell pepper**
2 tablespoons (21 g) **chopped black olives**
2 tablespoons (13 g) **sliced green onions**

2 tablespoons (17 g) **chopped green chiles**
2 teaspoons (10 g) **white vinegar**
¼ teaspoon (.7 g) **garlic powder**
⅛ teaspoon (.3 g) **freshly ground pepper**
¼ cup (28 g) **shredded low-fat sharp Cheddar cheese**

Cut 3 circles from each tortilla with biscuit cutter. Dip rounds in cold water; drain on paper towels. Place rounds in single layer on ungreased baking sheet. Bake at 350° F (177° C) for 10 minutes or until chips are crisp and beginning to brown. Cool. Mix tomato, green pepper, olives, green onions, chiles, vinegar, garlic powder and pepper in bowl. Spoon 2 teaspoons mixture onto each tortilla chip. Sprinkle equal amount of cheese over chips. Broil 6 inches (15 cm) from heat for 1 minute or until cheese melts.
Yield: 26 servings.

Gayle Williford, Jonesboro High School, Jonesboro, GA

Vegetable Pizza

1 large package **crescent rolls**
1 small package **crescent rolls**
8 ounces (227 g) **cream cheese, softened**
1 cup (221 g) **mayonnaise**
1 envelope **ranch salad dressing mix**

1 cup (100 g) **finely chopped cauliflower**
¾ cup (66 g) **finely chopped broccoli**
¾ cup (83 g) **grated carrots**
Bacon bits

Press rolls to cover bottom of 11x15-inch (27.5x37.5-cm) baking pan. Bake at 375° F (191° C) for 8 to 10 minutes or until browned. Cool completely. Blend cream cheese, mayonnaise and dressing mix in bowl. Spread over cooled crust. Sprinkle with vegetables. Top with bacon bits. Chill until serving time. Cut into bars. Yield: 15 to 20 servings.

Doris Stults, Collinwood High School, Collinwood, TN

Bite-Size Party Pizzas

6 tablespoons (85 g) **margarine,**
  softened
1 egg
1 cup plus 2 tablespoons (141 g)
  flour
¹/₂ cup (28 g) **crushed Corn Chex**
¹/₂ teaspoon (2.8 g) **salt**
¹/₄ cup (59 g) **water**

1 pound (454 g) **pork sausage**
1 (10-ounce) (284-g) **can pizza**
  sauce
1 teaspoon (2.8 g) **garlic powder**
2¹/₂ tablespoons (23 g) **sliced**
  pitted black olives
1¹/₂ cup (170 g) **shredded**
  mozzarella cheese

Beat butter in mixer bowl. Stir in egg. Add flour, cereal and salt gradually, beating until crumbly. Stir in water. Roll ¹/₄ inch (.75 cm) thick on lightly floured surface. Cut with 2¹/₂-inch (6.5-cm) biscuit cutter. Place on greased baking sheet. Bake at 400° F (204° C) for 10 to 13 minutes or until edges are lightly browned. Brown sausage in skillet; drain. Stir in pizza sauce and garlic powder. Bring to a boil; reduce heat. Simmer, covered, for 5 to 10 minutes. Place 1 tablespoon (35 g) sausage mixture, 2 olive slices and 1 tablespoon (7.1 g) cheese on each pizza round. Bake at 400° F (204° C) for 5 minutes or until cheese is melted. Yield: 24 servings.

Linda M. Sader, Beloit Jr.-Sr. High School, Beloit, KS

Snappy Stuffed Tomatillas

Use the current year of the Chinese calendar as a decorating theme for your New Year's Eve party.

20 tomatillas or cherry tomatoes
²/₃ cup (75 g) **shredded Cheddar**
  cheese
¹/₂ cup (308 g) **whole kernel corn**
2 green onions with tops, sliced

6 ounces (170 g) **cream cheese,**
  softened
1 teaspoon (3.1 g) **ground red**
  chiles

Cut thin slice from stem ends of tomatillas. Remove pulp and seeds with melon baller or spoon. Mix Cheddar cheese, corn, green onions, cream cheese and 1 teaspoon (3.1 g) red chiles. Fill tomatillas with cheese mixture. Sprinkle with ground chiles. Top with cilantro and green onions. Yield: 20 servings.

Sharen Hanson and Amanda Grue, Manhattan High School, Manhattan, MT

Sausage Balls

1 pound (454 g) **sausage**   **½ cup** (63 g) **flour**
1 package baking mix

Mix all ingredients in bowl. Shape into small balls. Place in baking dish. Bake at 400° F (204° C) for 10 to 12 minutes or until browned. Let stand to cool. Store in tightly covered container. Yield: 36 servings.

Bonnie Claycomb, Caverna High School, Horse Cave, KY

Sausage Squares

1 cup (113 g) **baking mix**   **2 tablespoons** (28 g) **mayonnaise**
⅓ cup (81 g) **milk**   **2 cups** (226 g) **shredded**
2 tablespoons (28 g) **mayonnaise**   **Cheddar cheese**
1 pound (454 g) **hot sausage**   **2 (4-ounce)** (113-g) **cans**
½ cup (80 g) **chopped onion**   **chopped green chiles**
1 egg

Mix baking mix, milk and 2 tablespoons (28 g) mayonnaise in bowl. Press into greased 9x13-inch (23x33-cm) baking dish. Sauté sausage with onion in skillet; drain on paper towels. Spread in baking dish. Beat egg with remaining 2 tablespoons (28 g) mayonnaise, cheese and chiles in bowl. Spread over sausage layer. Bake at 375° F (191° C) for 25 minutes. Cut into squares. Yield: 40 to 60 servings.

Kathie Perkinson, Bowling Green High School, Bowling Green, KY

A Party Hint

Use potted plants—placed in baskets, antique bowls or pitchers— as centerpieces for early spring get-togethers. "Recycle" them later in your flower garden, deck or somewhere outdoors.

Sausage Stars

1 package won ton wrappers
Vegetable oil
2 cups (200 g) cooked sausage,
   crumbled
1½ cups (170 g) shredded
   Monterey Jack cheese

1 cup (238 g) ranch salad
   dressing
1 cup (170 g) sliced olives
½ cup (50 g) chopped red
   pepper (optional)

Grease muffin cups. Press 1 won ton wrapper into each muffin cup. Brush with oil. Bake at 375° F (191° C) for 5 minutes or until golden brown. Remove from muffin cups and place on baking sheet. Combine remaining ingredients in bowl; mix well. Spoon into baked wrappers. Bake at 375° F (191° C) for 5 minutes. May prepare sausage mixture ahead and chill until 10 minutes before baking time. Yield: 48 to 60 servings.

Kim Winter, Andale High School, Andale, KS

Southwestern Appetizer

1 pound (454 g) ground beef
1 yellow onion, chopped
1 tablespoon (14 g) butter
1 (16-ounce) (454-g) can refried
   beans
1 (8-ounce) (227-g) jar medium
   taco sauce
2 cups (226 g) shredded
   Monterey Jack cheese
2 (4-ounce) (113-g) cans
   chopped green chiles, drained

2 cups (460 g) sour cream
6 ounces (170 g) cream cheese,
   softened
½ cup (118 g) Italian salad
   dressing
2 avocados, peeled, chopped
Sliced green onions
Chopped tomatoes
Sliced black olives
2 cups (226 g) shredded
   Monterey Jack cheese

Sauté ground beef with onion and butter in skillet until lightly browned; drain. Stir in beans and taco sauce. Cook until heated through. Spread on large platter. Top with 2 cups (226 g) shredded cheese. Sprinkle with chiles. Mix sour cream, cream cheese, salad dressing and avocados in bowl. Layer over chiles. Top with green onions, tomatoes, olives and remaining 2 cups (226 g) shredded cheese. Chill until serving time. Yield: 50 servings.

Diana Stewart, Moberly Public Schools, Moberly, MO

Shrimp Mold

1½ tablespoons (11 g)
  unflavored gelatin
½ cup (119 g) cold water
8 ounces (227 g) cream cheese
1 (10-ounce) (284-g) can tomato
  soup

1 cup (120 g) finely chopped
  celery
2 tablespoons (20 g) grated onion
1 cup (221 g) mayonnaise
1½ pounds (680 g) chopped
  boiled shrimp

Soften gelatin in cold water. Combine cream cheese with soup in saucepan. Cook until cream cheese is melted. Stir in celery, onion, mayonnaise and shrimp; mix well. Stir in gelatin mixture. Pour into mold sprayed with nonstick cooking spray. Chill overnight. Serve with club crackers. Yield: 30 servings.

Linda M. Gasperson
North Charleston High School, North Charleston, SC

Spinach Balls

2 (10-ounce) (284-g) packages
  frozen chopped spinach
1 small onion, finely chopped
2 cups (140 g) stuffing mix
½ cup (50 g) grated Parmesan
  cheese
4 eggs, beaten

¾ cup (170 g) melted butter
½ teaspoon (.7 g) thyme
1 clove of garlic, minced
½ teaspoon (2.8 g) salt
½ teaspoon (1 g) pepper
½ teaspoon (1.2 g) nutmeg

Cook spinach using package directions; drain thoroughly. Combine with remaining ingredients in bowl; mix well. Chill in freezer for 10 to 15 minutes. Shape into 1-inch (2.5-cm) balls. Freeze on a tray; remove to freezer-proof container. Place in shallow baking dish. Bake at 350° F (177° C) for 15 minutes or until lightly browned. May be baked without being frozen. Yield: 40 servings.

Mary Jean Woodward, Noe Middle School, Louisville, KY

Rage-of-the-Age Chili Dip

1 (8-ounce) (227-g) **container
   cream cheese, softened**
¼ cup (122 g) **milk**

1 tablespoon (10 g) **party dip
   chili mix**

Combine all ingredients; mix well. Chill. Serve with vegetable dippers or potato chips. Yield: 20 servings.

Variations: Add any of the following to cream cheese mixture: ½ cup (70 g) finely chopped ham and 2 teaspoons (10 g) prepared horseradish; ¼ cup (43 g) chopped stuffed green olives; one 4-ounce (113-g) can mushrooms, drained and chopped; 2 tablespoons (29 g) Italian dressing and 2 tablespoons (13 g) Parmesan cheese. Use as a dip or fill mushroom caps and broil until golden brown.

Chipped Beef Dip

2 cups (460 g) **sour cream**
2 cups (442 g) **mayonnaise**
1/2 **(8-ounce) (227-g) package**
  chipped beef
1 teaspoon (2.8 g) **Beau Monde**
  seasoning

1 1/2 teaspoons (1.6 g) **dillweed**
1/2 teaspoon (1 g) **onion powder**
1/2 teaspoon (3 g) **garlic salt**
1 **round loaf pumpernickel bread**
1 **round loaf rye bread**

Mix all ingredients except bread in bowl. Cut a well in center of pumpernickel bread. Spoon chipped beef mixture into well. Tear remaining bread into chunks and use for dipping. Yield: 50 servings.

Karen Rutler, Loganville High School, Loganville, GA

Easy Chipped Beef Dip

8 ounces (227 g) **cream cheese,**
  softened
1 **(8-ounce) (227-g) package**
  chipped beef
1/3 cup (33 g) **chopped green**
  onions

1 **(8-ounce) (227-g) can crushed**
  pineapple, drained
1/2 teaspoon (2 g) **seasoned salt**
1/4 cup (25 g) **chopped green bell**
  pepper (optional)

Combine cream cheese, beef, green onions, pineapple, salt and green pepper in bowl; mix well. Serve with assorted crackers. Yield: 35 servings.

Kristina Parsons, South Haven USD #509, South Haven, KS

Dried Beef Dip

1 **bunch green onions, tops only**
16 ounces (454 g) **cream cheese,**
  softened

1 **(10-ounce) (284-g) can**
  tomatoes with green chiles
1 **(2-ounce) (57-g) jar dried beef**

Chop tops only of green onions. Mix cream cheese with tomatoes in bowl. Stir in green onion tops. Add dried beef; mix well. Chill until serving time. Serve with vegetable dippers, chips or crackers. Yield: 25 servings.

Jodie Ellzey, L.V. Berkner High School, Richardson, TX

Boursin Cheese

32 ounces (907 g) cream cheese, softened
1/2 cup (30 g) finely minced parsley
1 cup (48 g) finely minced chives

3 to 6 large cloves of garlic, mashed
1 1/2 teaspoons (8.3 g) salt
1 1/2 teaspoons (3 g) pepper

Combine all ingredients in mixer bowl; beat well. Serve on crackers or deep-fried pita bread. Yield: 90 servings.

Robin Cogburn, Liberty High School, Spangle, WA

Black-Eyed Pea Dip, aka Texas Caviar

3 (15-ounce) (425-g) cans black eyed-peas, drained
1 (14-ounce) (397-g) can white hominy, drained
1 (2-ounce) (57-g) jar chopped pimento, drained
1 1/2 cups (150 g) chopped green or red bell pepper
3/4 cup (102 g) chopped jalapeños

2/3 cup (107 g) chopped purple onion
1 1/2 teaspoons (4.3 g) minced garlic
1 cup (235 g) Italian salad dressing
Salt to taste
1/8 teaspoon (.7 g) Tabasco sauce

Combine all ingredients in bowl; mix well. Chill, covered, in refrigerator for 3 to 7 days. Serve with tortilla chips. Garnish with carrot curls or strips. Yield: 15 to 20 servings.

Evelyn Langley, Llano High School, Llano, TX

A Party Hint

The more make-ahead, put-in-the-refrigerator recipes the better— less stress and more time for those special touches that make the occasion go "just as planned."

Black Olive Dip

1 (8-ounce) (227-g) can black
  olives, chopped
1 (8-ounce) (227-g) can tomatoes
  with green chiles, drained
1/4 cup (58 g) sour cream
1/2 pound (227 g) ground beef

3/4 cup (173 g) sour cream
1/2 cup (57 g) shredded Cheddar
  cheese
1/2 cup (53 g) shredded Monterey
  Jack cheese

Mix olives, tomatoes and 1/4 cup (58 g) sour cream in bowl. Spread in serving dish. Brown ground beef in skillet; drain. Spread over tomato mixture. Top with remaining 3/4 cup (173 g) sour cream. Sprinkle with mixture of Cheddar and Monterey Jack cheeses. Serve with chips. Yield: 10 to 12 servings.

Kandi L. Hammons, Fuller Jr. High School, Little Rock, AR

Hot Broccoli Dip

2 (10-ounce) (284-g) packages
  frozen chopped broccoli,
  thawed
1/4 cup (57 g) butter or margarine
2 cups (240 g) chopped celery
2 large onions, chopped
2 cloves of garlic, minced
2 (10-ounce) (284-g) cans cream
  of mushroom soup

16 ounces (454 g) cream cheese,
  softened
8 ounces (227 g) mild Mexican
  Velveeta cheese
Cayenne to taste
1/2 cup (68 g) slivered almonds
  (optional)

Cook broccoli using package directions; drain. Melt butter in large skillet. Add celery, onions, garlic and broccoli. Cook until tender. Combine cooked mixture with soup, cheeses and pepper in large saucepan. Cook until cheeses are melted and mixture is smooth, stirring frequently. Stir in almonds. Serve hot in chafing dish accompanied by corn chips. Yield: 50 to 75 servings.

Sandra Overman, West Hall Middle School, Oakwood, GA

Chicken Almond Spread

3 ounces (85 g) **cream cheese, softened**
1/2 teaspoon (1 g) **celery seeds**
1/2 teaspoon (1.1 g) **onion powder**
1 teaspoon (4 g) **seasoned salt**
1/8 teaspoon (.7 g) **Tabasco sauce**

1 teaspoon (5.7 g) **Worcestershire sauce**
1/3 cup (77 g) **sour cream**
1/4 cup (33 g) **chopped almonds**
1 cup (140 g) **chopped cooked chicken breast**

Combine all ingredients in bowl; mix well. Chill until serving time. Serve with crackers or canapé bread. Yield: 15 servings.

Delia E. Thomas, John C. Birdlebough High School, Phoenix, NY

Awesome Chili Dip

8 ounces (227 g) **Mexican Velveeta cheese**

1 (12-ounce) (340-g) **can chili without beans**

Place cheese in center of microwave-safe dish. Spoon chili over cheese. Microwave on High for 6 minutes or until cheese is melted, stirring once. Stir before serving. Serve with tortilla chips. Yield: 6 to 8 servings.

Lita Tabish, Deer Park High School, Deer Park, WA

Chili Con Queso Dip

1 pound (454 g) **ground chuck**
1 large onion, finely chopped
1 green bell pepper, chopped
1 teaspoon (5.5 g) **salt**
1/4 teaspoon (.5 g) **pepper**
1 teaspoon (2.8 g) **minced garlic**
1 teaspoon (6 g) **garlic salt**

1 tablespoon (7.5 g) **chili powder**
1 (8-ounce) (227-g) **jar Cheez Whiz**
8 ounces (227 g) **soft cream cheese**
1 (4-ounce) (113-g) **can chopped green chiles**

Brown ground chuck in skillet; drain. Add next 7 ingredients; mix well. Stir in cheeses and chiles. Spoon into slow cooker. Cook on Low for 2 hours. Serve with chips. Yield: 40 servings.

Jean M. Dutchess, Mt. Morris Central School, Mt. Morris, NY

Zesty Cheese Ball

8 ounces (227 g) cream cheese,
  softened
8 ounces (227 g) sharp Cheddar
  cheese, shredded
8 ounces (227 g) American
  cheese, shredded
2 tablespoons (13 g) chopped
  green bell pepper
White pepper to taste

2 tablespoons (20 g) grated onion
2 tablespoons (24 g) chopped
  pimento
2 tablespoons (34 g)
  Worcestershire sauce
1/2 teaspoon (3 g) soy sauce
1/2 teaspoon (2.6 g) Tabasco
  sauce
3/4 cup (89 g) chopped pecans

Mix all ingredients except pecans in bowl. Shape into 1 large ball or 2 smaller
balls. Chill, wrapped in plastic wrap, for 2 to 3 days to age. Roll in pecans.
Serve with a variety of crackers. Yield: 20 servings.

Myra McGee, Purdy R-II, Purdy, MO

Vegetable Cheese Ball

1 pound (454 g) Vermont white
  Cheddar cheese, shredded
8 ounces (227 g) cream cheese,
  softened
1/4 cup (25 g) finely chopped
  green bell pepper

2 tablespoons (20 g) finely
  chopped onion
1 to 2 tablespoons (15 to 31 g)
  milk
1 cup (119 g) chopped pecans

Combine cheese, cream cheese, green pepper and onion in mixer bowl. Mix
until smooth and well blended, adding milk if needed. Shape into large ball.
Roll in pecans. Serve with a variety of party crackers. Yield: 25 servings.

Mickey G. Weikle, Pulaski Middle School, Pulaski, VA

Bean Dip

2 (8-ounce) (227-g) cans bean dip
1 cup (230 g) sour cream
2 tablespoons (28 g)
  mayonnaise-type salad
  dressing
1 onion, chopped
1 tomato, chopped

2 slices bacon, crisp-fried,
  crumbled
8 ounces (227 g) Cheddar
  cheese, shredded
1 (4-ounce) (113-g) can black
  olives, sliced
1 large bag tortilla chips

Mix bean dip, sour cream and salad dressing in bowl. Spread on large serving platter. Top with onion, tomato, bacon, cheese and olives. Arrange chips around edge of platter. Serve immediately. May prepare bean dip mixture ahead and chill until serving time. Yield: 25 servings.

Karen Mason, East Newton High School, Cranby, MO

Cheese Ball

12 ounces (340 g) cream cheese,
  softened
1 (5-ounce) (142-g) jar Old
  English cheese
1/2 cup (60 g) chopped pecans

1 tablespoon (15 g) onion juice
2 teaspoons (11.3 g)
  Worcestershire sauce
1 bunch parsley, finely chopped
1/2 cup (60 g) chopped pecans

Combine cheeses, 1/2 cup (60 g) pecans, onion juice, Worcestershire sauce and parsley in bowl; mix well. Chill, covered, overnight. Shape into ball. Roll in remaining pecans. Serve with favorite small crackers. Yield: 25 servings.

Nancy Billings, Whitesburg Middle School

A Party Hint

Use a Mexican theme for your party. Decorate with colorful paper flowers, greet guests in Spanish, and provide plenty of large hats, pinatas and noise-makers.

Favorite Cheese Spread

1 envelope ranch dip mix
2 cups (460 g) sour cream
8 ounces (227 g) cream cheese,
  softened

8 ounces (227 g) Cheddar
  cheese, shredded
1/2 cup (60 g) chopped pecans

Combine dry dip mix with sour cream in bowl. Combine with cheeses and pecans in mixer bowl; mix well. Serve with chips or crackers.
Yield: 50 servings.

Kathy Wright, Northwood High School, Saltville, VA

Cheese Cucumber Spread

1 (8-ounce) (227-g) package
  cream cheese, softened
1/2 cup (104 g) drained shredded
  cucumber
1/4 cup (40 g) finely chopped
  onion

1 tablespoon (10 g) party dip
  chili mix
1 tablespoon (3.8 g) chopped
  parsley

Combine cream cheese and remaining ingredients in bowl; mix well. Serve with crackers, corn chips or potato chips. Yield: 20 servings.

Cream Cheese Dip

1 (8-ounce) (227-g) package
  cream cheese, softened
1 tablespoon (10 g) party dip
  chili mix

Salt and freshly ground pepper
  to taste

Heat cream cheese in a double boiler over hot water. Combine warmed cream cheese, party dip chili mix, salt and pepper in bowl; mix well. Serve with corn chips, potato chips or vegetable dippers. Also great on top of tacos and enchiladas. Yield: 20 servings.

Baked Crab Meat Dip

2 tablespoons (28 g) butter or margarine
1/2 cup (50 g) chopped red bell pepper
2 tablespoons (13 g) sliced green onions or 1 1/2 teaspoons (3.3 g) onion powder
1 clove of garlic, minced
2 tablespoons (16 g) flour
1/4 teaspoon (.6 g) white pepper
1 cup (244 g) milk
1/4 cup (25 g) grated Parmesan cheese
1/2 cup (68 g) frozen or canned cooked crab meat
1 ounce (28 g) Cheddar cheese, shredded

Melt butter in skillet over medium heat. Add red pepper, green onions and garlic. Cook for 2 to 3 minutes or until tender, stirring constantly. Stir in flour and white pepper. Cook for 1 minute. Add milk gradually. Bring to a boil, stirring constantly. Stir in Parmesan cheese; remove from heat. Stir in crab meat. Pour into greased 9-inch (23-cm) pie plate. Sprinkle with Cheddar cheese. Bake at 350° F (177° C) for 10 to 15 minutes or until mixture is heated through and cheese is melted. Serve with Melba toast rounds or crackers. Yield: 20 servings.

Delia E. Thomas, John C. Birdlebough High School, Phoenix, NY

Creamy Picante Pecan Dip

8 ounces (227 g) cream cheese, softened
1 (12-ounce) (340-g) jar mild picante sauce
1 cup (230 g) sour cream
3/4 cup (89 g) chopped pecans
1 cup (100 g) minced green onions (optional)
1/2 cup (50 g) finely chopped red bell peppers

Mix cream cheese with picante sauce in bowl. Add sour cream, pecans, green onions and red peppers; mix with wooden spoon until of creamy consistency. Yield: 15 servings.

Pat Brodeen, Theodore Roosevelt School, San Antonio, TX

Pizza Pie Crab Dip

8 ounces (227 g) **cream cheese,
 softened
1 tablespoon** (17 g)
 **Worcestershire sauce
1 small onion, grated**

¹/₈ teaspoon (.7 g) **salt
2 tablespoons** (28 g) **mayonnaise
¹/₂ (12-ounce)** (340-g) **bottle chili
 sauce
1 (6-ounce)** (170-g) **can crab meat**

Combine cream cheese, Worcestershire sauce, onion, salt and mayonnaise in bowl; mix well. Spread on 10-inch (25-cm) plate or pizza pan. Spread with chili sauce. Sprinkle crab meat over top. Garnish with parsley. Chill for 2 hours or longer. Serve with crackers. Yield: 20 servings.

Joanne Julien, Lowell High School, Lowell, MA

Delicious Dip

2 (6-ounce) (170-g) **jars
 marinated artichoke hearts
1 (8-ounce)** (227-g) **jar non-
 marinated artichoke hearts
1 (8-ounce)** (227-g) **can chopped
 Ortega chiles**

¹/₄ cup (55 g) **(or more)
 mayonnaise
¹/₄ cup** (28 g) **(or more) shredded
 Monterey Jack cheese
¹/₄ cup** (28 g) **(or more) shredded
 sharp Cheddar cheese**

Break artichoke hearts into pieces. Arrange in 9x13-inch (23x33-cm) baking dish. Top with chiles. Spread with mayonnaise. Sprinkle with cheese. Bake at 350° F (177° C) for 25 minutes. Serve with tortilla chips or corn chips. Yield: 25 servings.

Thelma Robertson, Bryant Jr. High School, Bryant, AR

Easy Fruit Dip

8 ounces (227 g) **cream cheese, softened**

1 (7-ounce) (198-g) **jar marshmallow creme**

Blend cream cheese with marshmallow creme in bowl until smooth and creamy. Serve with favorite fresh fruit. Yield: 20 servings.

Connie Massey, Smith County High School, Carthage, TN

Fruit Dip

1 (16-ounce) (454-g) **can pineapple chunks**
1 (4-ounce) (113-g) **package pistachio instant pudding mix**

12 ounces (340 g) **whipped topping**

Drain pineapple and set aside. Combine juice with pudding mix in bowl; stir until pudding mix is dissolved. Let stand until thickened. Fold in whipped topping. Chill until serving time. Use as a dip for pineapple and other favorite bite-size fruit pieces. Yield: 25 servings.

Wanda Ingle, Floyd County High School, Floyd, VA

Southwest-Style Guacamole Dip

1 (8-ounce) (227-g) **package cream cheese, softened**
2 medium avocados, peeled, mashed
1/4 cup (40 g) **finely chopped onion**

1 tablespoon (15 g) **lemon juice**
1 tablespoon (10 g) **party dip chili mix**
1 cup (180 g) **chopped tomato**

Combine cream cheese, avocados, onion, lemon juice and party dip chili mix in bowl; mix well. Add tomato; mix lightly. Serve with corn chips, crisply fried tortillas, crackers or potato chips. Excellent with tacos, enchiladas, fajitas and tostadas. Yield: 30 servings.

Lulu Paste

2 eggs, beaten
3 tablespoons (45 g) vinegar
3 tablespoons (38 g) sugar
1/2 teaspoon (2.8 g) salt
8 ounces (227 g) cream cheese

3 tablespoons (43 g) melted butter
1/2 large green bell pepper, chopped
1 onion, chopped

Combine eggs, vinegar, sugar and salt in double boiler. Cook over hot water until thickened, stirring frequently. Add cream cheese, butter, green pepper and onion; mix well. Chill for 24 hours. Serve on crackers. Yield: 15 servings.

Linda Ford, Harrisburg High School, Harrisburg, AR

Peppery Dip with Vegetables

1 cup (221 g) mayonnaise
2 tablespoons (20 g) grated onion
2 teaspoons (10 g) tarragon vinegar
2 teaspoons (2 g) chopped fresh chives

2 teaspoons (11 g) chili sauce
1/2 teaspoon (1 g) curry powder
1/2 teaspoon (2.8 g) salt
1/4 teaspoon (.5 g) pepper
1/8 teaspoon (.2 g) ground thyme

Combine all ingredients in bowl; mix well. Chill, covered, until serving time. Serve with favorite fresh vegetables. Yield: 15 servings.

Mary M. McGee, Crescent High School, Iva, SC

Russian Dip

2 cups (442 g) mayonnaise
1/4 cup (63 g) hot barbecue sauce

Drained chopped pickles to taste

Combine mayonnaise, barbecue sauce and pickles in bowl; mix well. Yield: 15 servings.

Jean M. Dutchess, Mt. Morris Central School, Mt. Morris, NY

Salsa

1 (4-ounce) (113-g) can chopped
   black olives
1 (4-ounce) (113-g) can chopped
   green chiles
3 to 4 green onions, chopped

1 large tomato, chopped
Salt, pepper and garlic powder
   to taste
2 tablespoons (30 g) cider vinegar
3 tablespoons (41 g) olive oil

Combine olives, chiles, green onions, tomato and spices in bowl; mix well.
Stir in vinegar and olive oil. Chill until serving time. Serve with corn chips.
Yield: 10 servings.

Judith Greene, Lloyd C. Bird High School, Chesterfield, VA

Taco Dip

1 pound (454 g) lean ground beef
1 onion, chopped
1 (16-ounce) (454-g) can refried
   beans
1 (4-ounce) (113-g) jar
   medium-hot salsa
2 envelopes taco seasoning mix
1¹/₂ cups (170 g) shredded
   Cheddar cheese

1 cup (230 g) sour cream
¹/₂ cup (57 g) shredded Cheddar
   cheese
1 cup (56 g) shredded lettuce
   (optional)
1 tomato, chopped (optional)

Brown ground beef in skillet, stirring until crumbly; drain. Add onion. Cook
until tender. Add beans, salsa and taco seasoning mix. Spoon into 9x12-inch
(23x30-cm) baking dish. Top with 1¹/₂ cups (170 g) cheese. Bake at 350° F
(177° C) for 15 minutes. Top with sour cream, ¹/₂ cup (57 g) cheese, lettuce
and tomato. Serve with nacho chips. Yield: 12 servings.

Anita McCarty, Northside High School, Roanoke, VA

Easy Taco Dip

16 ounces (454 g) cream cheese,
  softened
1 (8-ounce) (227-g) jar picante
  sauce
Several finely torn lettuce leaves
1 tomato, finely chopped

1 (4-ounce) (113-g) can sliced
  black olives, drained
1 bunch green onions, thinly
  sliced
2 cups (226 g) shredded
  mozzarella cheese

Mix cream cheese with picante sauce in bowl. Spread on serving platter. Layer remaining ingredients in order given over cream cheese mixture. Serve with tortilla chips. Yield: 20 servings.

Alice F. Carter, Bleckley County High School, Cochran, GA

Tex-Mex Dip

1 or 2 (16-ounce) (454-g) cans
  bean dip
1½ cups (345 g) sour cream
2 ripe avocados, mashed
2 teaspoons (10 g) lemon or lime
  juice
2 tomatoes, chopped
1 bunch green onions with tops,
  thinly sliced

1 (4-ounce) (113-g) can chopped
  green chiles
1 (4-ounce) (113-g) can sliced
  black olives
8 ounces (227 g) Cheddar
  cheese, shredded

Spread bean dip on large round platter. Top with sour cream. Spread with mixture of avocados and lemon juice. Layer remaining ingredients over avocado mixture in order given. Serve with corn chips or Mexican-style chips. Yield: 30 servings.

Monica Smith, A & M Consolidated, College Station, TX

Favorite Tex-Mex Dip

1 (15-ounce) (425-g) can
  ranch-style beans, mashed
3 avocados, mashed
2 tablespoons (31 g) lemon juice
1/2 cup (110 g) mayonnaise
2 cups (460 g) sour cream
1 envelope taco seasoning mix

1 bunch green onions, chopped
2 (4-ounce) (113-g) cans
  chopped green chiles
3 tomatoes, peeled, seeded,
  chopped
8 ounces (227 g) Cheddar
  cheese, finely shredded

Spread beans on 10-inch (25-cm) plate. Mix avocados, lemon juice and mayonnaise in bowl. Spread over beans. Mix sour cream with seasoning mix in bowl. Spread over avocado mixture. Layer remaining ingredients over sour cream mixture in order given. Yield: 15 to 20 servings.

Teresa Morgan, Duncanville Ninth Grade, Dallas, TX

Fresh Vegetable Chili Spread

8 ounces (227 g) cream cheese,
  softened
1/2 cup (55 g) shredded carrot
1/2 cup (130 g) shredded zucchini

1 tablespoon (10 g) party dip
  chili mix
1 tablespoon (3.8 g) chopped
  parsley

Combine all ingredients in bowl; mix well. Serve with bread slices or assorted crackers. Yield: 30 servings.

Zucchini Dip

8 ounces (227 g) cream cheese,
  softened
3 tablespoons (46 g) milk
1 tablespoon (10 g) party dip
  chili mix

1 small zucchini, shredded
3 tablespoons (9 g) chopped
  chives

Combine cream cheese and milk in bowl; mix well. Add remaining ingredients; mix well. Chill. Serve with vegetable dippers or chips. Yield: 20 servings.

Easy Party Punch

To make a pretty ice ring for this punch, I arrange orange slices and whole cherries in a bundt pan and pour some of the punch mixture (before ginger ale is added) into the pan to freeze.

**1 envelope cherry-flavor drink
    mix**
**1 envelope strawberry-flavor
    drink mix**
2 cups (400 g) sugar
**1 (3-ounce) (85-g) can frozen
    orange juice concentrate**

**1 (3-ounce) (85-g) can frozen
    lemonade concentrate**
2 cups (474 g) hot water
10 cups (2370 g) water
1 quart (976 g) ginger ale

Dissolve drink mix, sugar and concentrates in 2 cups (474 g) hot water. Add remaining water. Chill until serving time. Add ginger ale.
Yield: 24 to 30 servings.

Vickie Bruce, Lake Hamilton Jr. High School, Pearcy, AR

Frosted Cocktail

¹/₂ cup (100 g) sugar	2 tablespoons (31 g) lime juice
²/₃ cup (158 g) water	2 egg whites
²/₃ cup (163 g) lemon juice	4 cups (1896 g) finely crushed ice
²/₃ cup (163 g) pineapple juice	

Combine sugar and water in saucepan. Cook for 5 minutes, stirring frequently. Chill thoroughly. Add remaining ingredients; mix well. Pour half the mixture into blender container. Process for 7 to 8 seconds or until light and frothy. Repeat with remaining mixture. Serve at once in chilled cocktail glasses with short straws. Yield: 8 to 10 servings.

Eric Veca, Three Forks, MT

Frosty Lime Fizz

1 (12-ounce) (340-g) can pineapple juice	1 quart (768 g) lime sherbet
¹/₂ cup (123 g) lime juice	1 (28-ounce) (794-g) bottle lemon-lime soda, chilled
¹/₂ cup (100 g) sugar	

Combine first 3 ingredients and half the sherbet in blender container. Process until smooth. Pour ¹/₂ cup (105 g) into each of 6 large glasses. Add scoop of remaining sherbet to each glass. Fill with soda. Yield: 6 servings.

Amy Bakeberg and Luke Miest, Manhattan High School, Manhattan, MT

Fruit Punch

1 (6-ounce) (170-g) can each frozen orange juice and lemonade concentrate	1 cup (200 g) sugar
1 (46-ounce) (1304-g) can pineapple juice	1 tablespoon (14 g) almond extract
	1 (1-liter) bottle ginger ale

Prepare concentrates using package directions. Combine with next 3 ingredients in large container; mix well. Chill. Stir in ginger ale. Yield: 30 servings.

Jane Acevedo, Starr-Iva Middle School, Starr, SC

Grand Glorious Punch

1 (3-ounce) (85-g) package
   cherry gelatin
1 cup (237 g) boiling water
1 (6-ounce) (170-g) can frozen
   lemonade or pineapple-orange
   juice concentrate

3 cups (711 g) cold water
1 (1-quart) (1-liter) bottle
   cranberry juice cocktail, chilled
1 (12-ounce) (340-g) bottle
   ginger ale, chilled

Dissolve gelatin in boiling water. Stir in concentrate. Add cold water and juice cocktail; mix well. Pour over 2 trays of ice cubes or ice ring in punch bowl. Pour in ginger ale. Yield: 25 servings.

Linda Wall, Glenwood Jr. High School, Princeton, WV

Lime Icebergs

2 (7-ounce) (198-g) bottles
   lemon-lime soda
2 tablespoons (31 g) lime juice
2 to 3 drops of green food
   coloring

1 egg white
1 tablespoon (13 g) sugar

Mix soda, lime juice and food coloring in bowl. Freeze in 1-quart (1-liter) refrigerator tray just until slushy. Beat egg white in mixer bowl until soft peaks form. Add sugar gradually, beating until soft peaks form. Fold into lime mixture. Freeze until firm, stirring once. Break up with fork. Spoon into sherbet glasses. Garnish with lime wedges and mint sprigs.
Yield: 8 to 10 servings.

Danna Steindorf and Melanie Chaney
Manhattan High School, Manhattan, MT

Open-Your-Eyes Punch

This sharp tangy punch can be sweetened a bit by adding 1 cup (250 g) sweetened pineapple juice. All the caffeine in the punch is guaranteed to liven up any party occasion!

1 (12-ounce) (340-g) **can frozen
orange juice concentrate**

2 (2-liter) bottles Mountain Dew
5 pounds crushed ice

Place frozen concentrate in punch bowl; mash with ladle. Add soda and ice. Yield: 24 servings.

Juanita Fountain, Pisgah High School, Canton, NC

Party Punch

1 cup (200 g) **sugar**
2 quarts (1896 g) **water**
2 large cans reconstituted
    lemonade

2 large cans reconstituted
    orange juice
2 cups (500 g) **pineapple juice**
2 bottles ginger ale

Bring sugar and water to a boil in saucepan. Simmer for 5 minutes, stirring frequently. Cool to room temperature. Combine juices and ginger ale in large container; mix well. Freeze in clean 1-liter soda bottles until serving time. Pour partially thawed punch into punch bowl. Yield: 30 to 40 servings.

M. C. Potter, Bay High School, Bay, AR

Pink Lady Punch

1 quart (1012 g) **cranberry juice**
1 large can pineapple juice

2 liters ginger ale
1 1/2 cups (300 g) **sugar**

Combine all ingredients in large container; mix well. May chill or freeze for several days before serving. Yield: 20 servings.

Sandra Odom, Bald Knob High School, Bald Knob, AR

Red Punch

2 (3-ounce) (85-g) packages
  lemon gelatin
4 cups (800 g) sugar
4 cups (948 g) boiling water
1 (6-ounce) (170-g) can orange
  juice concentrate, diluted

1 large can pineapple juice
1 (46-ounce) (1304-g) can
  Hawaiian punch
Ginger ale

Dissolve gelatin and sugar in boiling water in bowl. Add juices and Hawaiian punch; mix well. Freeze in freezer-proof containers. Defrost to slushy stage. Pour into punch bowl. Add one 2-liter bottle of ginger ale per gallon (4 liters) of punch mixture. Yield: 30 servings.

Jeannette Lewallen, Franklin County High School, Carnesville, GA

Secret-Ingredient Punch

4 cups (800 g) sugar
6 cups (1422 g) hot water
2 (3-ounce) (85 g) packages
  lemon gelatin
1 (46-ounce) (1304-g) can
  pineapple juice

1 (1-ounce) (28-g) bottle almond
  extract
1 (6-ounce) (170-g) can frozen
  lemonade concentrate
2 to 3 bottles ginger ale

Bring sugar and 2 cups (474 g) of the water to a boil in saucepan. Cook until sugar is dissolved, stirring frequently. Pour into large bowl. Add 4 cups (948 g) hot water and gelatin; mix until gelatin is dissolved. Add pineapple juice, flavoring and concentrate; mix well. Pour into sealable plastic freezer bags. Freeze until firm. Scoop frozen mixture into chilled punch bowl. Stir in ginger ale; punch will be slushy. Yield: 30 to 40 servings.

Shelley Kilcrease, Kerens High School, Kerens, TX

Southern Tea Punch

3 lemons
6 cups (1422 g) water
2 cups (400 g) sugar
1½ teaspoons (7 g) vanilla
  extract
1½ teaspoons (7 g) almond
  extract

4 single-serving tea bags
4 cups (948 g) boiling water
2 (46-ounce) (1304-g) cans
  pineapple juice

Juice lemons and set aside. Combine lemon rinds, 6 cups (1422 g) water and sugar in saucepan. Bring to a boil. Simmer for 5 minutes, stirring frequently; remove rinds. Stir in flavorings and lemon juice. Steep tea bags in boiling water; remove tea bags. Combine tea, sugar mixture and pineapple juice in large container; mix well. Garnish with fresh mint. Yield: 20 to 30 servings.

Gloria H. Rawlston, Soddy-Daisy High School, Soddy-Daisy, TN

Special Punch

2 (6-ounce) (170-g) packages
  raspberry gelatin
3 cups (711 g) boiling water
3 (46-ounce) (1304-g) cans
  pineapple juice
½ gallon (1984 g) orange juice

3 envelopes presweetened
  lemonade mix
¾ cup (150 g) sugar
2 (2-liter) bottles ginger ale
½ gallon (1536 g) pineapple
  sherbet

Dissolve gelatin in hot water. Add juices, lemonade mix and sugar; mix well. Chill until serving time. Pour into punch bowl. Stir in ginger ale. Add sherbet in scoops at serving time. Yield: 50 servings.

Jan Russell, Pickett County High School, Byrdstown, TN

Special Wedding Punch

Food coloring to match the color scheme of the wedding may be added to this punch.

1 (12-ounce) (340-g) can frozen orange juice concentrate
2 (12-ounce) (340-g) cans frozen lemonade concentrate
4 juice cans water
1 (6-ounce) (170-g) can frozen limeade concentrate
1 (46-ounce) (1304-g) can pineapple juice
1/4 cup (62 g) maraschino cherry juice
1 tablespoon (14 g) almond extract
1/2 gallon (1536 g) raspberry or pineapple sherbet
2 quarts (2 liters) ginger ale

Combine orange juice and lemonade concentrates, water, limeade concentrate, pineapple juice, cherry juice and flavoring in 1-gallon (4-liter) container; mix well. Freeze in 1/2-gallon (2-liter) containers. Allow mixture to thaw slightly. Mix each 1/2-gallon (2-liter) frozen punch with 1 quart (768 g) sherbet and 1 quart (1 liter) ginger ale. Yield: 60 servings.

Nancy A. Marrow, East Rowan High School, Salisburg, NC

Strawberry-Banana Julius

1 (10-ounce) (284-g) package frozen strawberries
1 large banana, sliced
1 cup (244 g) milk
1 cup (237 g) cold water
1 teaspoon (4.8 g) vanilla extract
1/3 cup (67 g) sugar
10 to 12 ice cubes

Combine all ingredients in blender container. Process until smooth. Serve immediately. Yield: 6 servings.

Sandra S. Smith, Roosevelt Middle School, Springfield, OH

Sunny Day Punch

1 (12-ounce) (-g) can frozen
   orange juice concentrate
1 (12-ounce) (-g) can frozen
   lemonade concentrate

3 cups (750 g) **pineapple juice**
4 cups (948 g) **water**
2 bottles ginger ale

Combine concentrates, pineapple juice and water in bowl; mix well. Chill until serving time. Stir in ginger ale. Garnish with orange slices.
Yield: 25 servings.

Jeannette Lewallen, Franklin County High School, Carnesville, GA

Hot Mulled Cider

1 orange
Whole cloves
1 cup (181 g) packed brown
   sugar
2 teaspoons (4 g) whole allspice
2 teaspoons (2.2 g) whole cloves

1/3 teaspoon (1.8 g) salt
1/8 teaspoon (.3 g) nutmeg
2 (3-inch) (7.5-cm) cinnamon
   sticks
1 gallon (4 liters) apple cider

Cut orange into wedges; insert 1 whole clove into each wedge. Combine remaining ingredients in saucepan. Bring to a boil slowly. Simmer, covered, for 20 minutes. Remove spices with slotted spoon. Serve in warmed mugs garnished with orange wedges. Yield: 12 to 16 servings.

Esther Keithley, Pierce City High School, Pierce City, MO

Slow-Cooker Hot Mulled Cider

Whole cloves
1 large orange

1 gallon (4 liters) apple cider

Insert cloves into orange, completely covering orange. Place in baking dish. Bake at 300° F (149° C) for 2 hours. Place in slow cooker. Pour in cider. Cook on Low for 1 hour. Serve with cinnamon stick. Yield: 15 servings.

Lynne G. Pritchett, Gilmer High School, Ellijay, GA

Spook 'n' Cider

10 cups (2480 g) **apple cider or apple juice**
1 (5-inch) (13-cm) **cinnamon stick**

1 (12-ounce) (340-g) **package lightly sweetened frozen strawberries or red raspberries**

Combine apple juice, cinnamon and strawberries in large saucepan. Bring to a boil; reduce heat. Simmer, covered, for 10 minutes; remove from heat. Strain berries and cinnamon from mixture. Let cider stand, covered, until serving time. Reheat to serve. Yield: 16 servings.

Glynda Hooper, Marlow High School, Marlow, OK

Witch's Brew

2 cups (474 g) **water**
1/2 cup (100 g) **sugar**
2 1/2 cups (620 g) **orange juice**
1 cup (250 g) **pineapple juice**

1 1/2 teaspoons (3 g) **grated lemon rind**
6 cups (1240 g) **chilled apple cider**

Combine water and sugar in saucepan. Cook over medium heat until sugar is dissolved. Cool completely. Stir in juices and lemon rind. Chill, covered, until serving time. Stir in cider. Yield: 12 servings.

Jean Keenan, William Byrd Middle School, Vinton, VA

A Party Hint

Freeze some of the punch or beverage in a ring mold or in ice cube trays to chill the punch without diluting it.

Soup
to
Nuts

Soups and Salads

Corn and Pepper Chowder

1 **teaspoon** (4.5 g) **olive oil**
1 **cup** (160 g) **chopped onion**
1 **cup** (100 g) **red bell pepper**
5 **teaspoons** (13 g) **flour**
¹/₂ **teaspoon** (1.1 g) **ground cumin**
¹/₈ **teaspoon** (.2 g) **red pepper**
¹/₂ **pound** (227 g) **red potatoes, peeled, chopped**
2 **cups** (474 g) **water**

1 **teaspoon** (4.8 g) **instant chicken bouillon**
2 **cups** (328 g) **frozen whole kernel corn, thawed**
2 **tablespoons** (17 g) **drained canned chopped green chiles**
1 **cup** (245 g) **evaporated skim milk**
¹/₄ **teaspoon** (.5 g) **black pepper**

Heat oil in Dutch oven over medium-high heat. Add onion and bell pepper. Sauté for 5 minutes, stirring frequently. Stir in flour, cumin and red pepper. Cook for 1 minute. Add potatoes, water and bouillon. Bring to a boil, stirring frequently; reduce heat. Simmer, covered, for 10 minutes or until potatoes are tender and liquid is thickened. Add remaining ingredients. Bring to a boil over medium heat. Serve hot. Yield: 8 to 10 servings.

Kevin Nelson, Bloomingdale High School, Bloomingdale, MI

Chili Chicken Gumbo

1 (28-ounce) (794-g) can tomatoes
1½ cups (356 g) water
1 whole chicken breast, boned,
   skinned, cut into 1½-inch
   (4-cm) pieces
½ pound (227 g) ham, cut into
   ¾-inch (2.25-cm) cubes
¾ cup (120 g) chopped onion
¾ cup (90 g) sliced celery
1 clove of garlic, minced

½ teaspoon (.1 g) thyme leaves
1 envelope party dip chili mix
3 tablespoons (23 g) flour
1 pound (454 g) shrimp, peeled,
   deveined
1 large green bell pepper, cut
   into ¾-inch (2.25-cm) pieces
¼ cup (15 g) minced parsley
3 cups (615 g) hot cooked rice,
   prepared in chicken broth

Drain and coarsely chop tomatoes, reserving juice. Combine water, tomatoes, juice and next 6 ingredients in large skillet. Bring to a boil; reduce heat and cover. Simmer for 15 minutes. Combine party dip chili mix and flour; mix well. Add to skillet with shrimp and green pepper. Cook, uncovered, for 5 minutes or until shrimp are cooked through and gumbo is thickened. Stir parsley into rice. Ladle gumbo into bowls; top with rice. Yield: 6 to 7 servings.

Steve's Jambalaya

1 (4-pound) (1814-g) chicken
½ cup (60 g) chopped celery
1 teaspoon (5.5 g) salt
½ teaspoon (1.1 g) black pepper
1 pound (454 g) hot sausage
1 pound (454 g) sliced link
   sausage
2 bunches green onions, chopped

4½ cups (1067 g) broth or water
1 small package wild rice with
   seasoning packet
⅛ teaspoon (.2 g) red pepper
⅛ teaspoon (.4 g) garlic powder
Creole and Louisiana hot sauces
   to taste
1 cup (185 g) rice

Combine first 4 ingredients with water to cover in large pot. Bring to a boil; reduce heat. Simmer for 20 minutes until chicken is tender. Debone and chop cooled chicken; set aside. Brown sausages in skillet; drain. Add green onions. Cook over low heat until brown, stirring occasionally. Combine chicken, sausage mixture and broth in large pot. Add seasoning packet, red pepper, garlic powder and hot sauces. Bring to a boil. Add rice. Simmer, covered, until liquid is absorbed. Yield: 10 to 12 servings.

Monnita Brasher, Lancaster High School, Lancaster, TX

Cheesy Potato Soup

A steaming mug hits the spot after an afternoon or evening of snow fun.

1 cup (160 g) chopped onion
2 tablespoons (28 g) margarine
2 cups (244 g) thinly sliced
  potatoes
1 (10-ounce) (284-g) can cream
  of chicken soup

1 cup (244 g) milk
Salt and pepper to taste
8 ounces (227 g) Cheddar
  cheese, shredded

Sauté onion in margarine in saucepan. Add potatoes and water to cover. Cook for 5 to 10 minutes or until potatoes are tender. Add soup, milk and seasonings. Cook until heated through. Add cheese. Cook until cheese is melted. Yield: 4 servings.

Linda W. Kelly, Smyth County Vocational School, Marion, VA

Christmas Gelatin Salad

1 (20-ounce) (567-g) can
  pineapple slices
2³/₄ cups (652 g) water
1 (6-ounce) (170-g) package
  lemon gelatin
10 maraschino cherries

2¹/₄ cups (563 g) pineapple juice
1 (6-ounce) (170-g) package
  strawberry gelatin
1 (16-ounce) (454-g) can whole
  cranberry sauce

Drain pineapple, reserving ³/₄ cup (188 g) juice. Bring reserved juice and water to a boil in saucepan. Stir in lemon gelatin until dissolved. Chill until slightly thickened. Spoon 1 cup (524 g) into shallow 2-quart (2-liter) mold. Arrange pineapple slices on top. Insert 1 cherry into center of each slice. Pour remaining gelatin over slices. Chill until almost set. Bring 2¹/₄ cups (563 g) pineapple juice to a boil in saucepan. Stir in strawberry gelatin until dissolved. Chill until slightly thickened. Stir in cranberry sauce. Spoon over lemon gelatin. Chill overnight or until firm. Yield: 16 servings.

LaDell Emmons, McAlester High School, McAlester, OK

Holiday Salad

1 (3-ounce) (85-g) package
  orange gelatin
1 (3-ounce) (85-g) package
  cherry gelatin
1 cup (237 g) boiling water

1 small can crushed pineapple
1 (6-ounce) (170-g) can frozen
  orange juice concentrate
1 (16-ounce) (454-g) can whole
  cranberry sauce

Dissolve gelatins in boiling water in bowl. Add remaining ingredients; mix well. Pour into 9x9-inch (23x23-cm) pan. Chill until firm. Yield: 8 to 12 servings.

Nancy Billings, Whitesburg Middle School

Party Chicken Salad

1 (8-ounce) (227-g) can crushed
  pineapple
8 ounces (227 g) cream cheese,
  softened
2 tablespoons (20 g) party dip
  chili mix
2 cups (280 g) chopped cooked
  chicken
1 (6-ounce) (170-g) can water
  chestnuts, drained, sliced

1/2 cup (60 g) celery slices
1/4 cup (25 g) green onion slices
1/4 cup (34 g) toasted slivered
  almonds
1/4 teaspoon (1.4 g) salt
Dash of pepper
4 medium tomatoes

Drain pineapple, reserving syrup. Combine reserved syrup, cream cheese and party dip chili mix in bowl; mix well. Add pineapple, chicken, water chestnuts, celery, green onions, almonds, salt and pepper; mix lightly. Chill in refrigerator. Cut each tomato into six sections to but not through stem end. Fill with chicken salad. Yield: 4 servings.

Corn Bread Salad

1 envelope ranch salad dressing
  mix
1 cup (230 g) sour cream
1 cup (221 g) mayonnaise
3 large tomatoes, chopped
1/2 cup (50 g) chopped green bell
  pepper
1/2 cup (50 g) chopped green
  onions

1 (9-inch) (23-cm) pan corn bread
2 (16-ounce) (454-g) cans pinto
  beans, drained
2 cups (226 g) shredded
  Cheddar cheese
10 slices bacon, crisp-fried,
  crumbled
2 (17-ounce) (482-g) cans whole
  kernel corn, drained

Mix salad dressing mix, sour cream and mayonnaise in small bowl; set aside. Mix tomatoes, green pepper and green onions in medium bowl; set aside. Layer corn bread, beans, tomato mixture, cheese, bacon, corn and mayonnaise mixture 1/2 at a time in large serving bowl. Chill, covered, for 2 to 3 hours. Yield: 10 to 12 servings.

Sandra Odom, Bald Knob High School, Bald Knob, AR

Garlic Dressing

8 ounces (227 g) cream cheese,
  softened
1/2 cup (115 g) sour cream
1 tablespoon (10 g) party dip
  chili mix

1/4 cup (61 g) milk
1 teaspoon (5.1 g) lemon juice
1 clove of garlic, minced

Combine cream cheese, sour cream, party dip chili mix, milk, lemon juice and garlic in mixer bowl; mix well. Chill. Serve with vegetables and main dish salads. Yield: 10 servings.

Zingy Potato Salad

4 cups (624 g) **chopped cooked potatoes**
1/2 cup (60 g) **celery slices**
8 slices **bacon, crisp-fried, crumbled**
1/4 cup (25 g) **grated Parmesan cheese**

2 tablespoons (20 g) **party dip chili mix**
2 tablespoons (13 g) **chopped green onions**
1/3 cup (78 g) **Italian dressing**
8 ounces (227 g) **cream cheese, softened**

Combine potatoes, celery, bacon, Parmesan cheese, party dip chili mix and green onions in bowl; mix lightly. Add dressing to cream cheese gradually, mixing well after each addition. Pour over potato mixture; mix lightly. Spoon and gently press mixture into lightly oiled ring mold. Chill for several hours or overnight. Unmold onto serving plate. Yield: 8 servings.

Salmon and Rice Salad

1 cup (144 g) **frozen peas, thawed**
2 cups (410 g) **cooked rice**
1 cup (120 g) **sliced celery**
1/2 cup (50 g) **sliced green onions**
1/2 cup (123 g) **sweet pickle relish**
1/2 to 1 cup (110 to 221 g) **mayonnaise-type salad dressing**

1/2 teaspoon (1 g) **pepper**
1 or 2 (6-ounce) (170-g) **cans pink salmon**
1/2 cup (50 g) **chopped red bell pepper**
1/2 cup (69 g) **pine nuts**

Microwave peas for 2 to 3 minutes or until slightly cooked. Combine with remaining ingredients in bowl; toss gently. Chill until serving time. Serve on lettuce leaves. Yield: 6 servings.

Janice Lee, Rockdale ISO, Rockdale, TX

Main Dishes

Fancy Barbecue Beef

¹/₂ cup (119 g) **dry white wine**
¹/₄ cup (61 g) **catsup**
1 tablespoon (16 g) **prepared mustard**
¹/₄ to ³/₈ teaspoon (1.3 to 2 g) **Tabasco sauce**
Pepper to taste

2 large onions, cut into quarters
¹/₂ cup (35 g) **sliced mushrooms (optional)**
¹/₄ cup (45 g) **packed brown sugar**
1¹/₂ pounds (680 g) **sirloin cubes**

Combine wine, catsup, mustard, Tabasco sauce, pepper, onions, mushrooms and brown sugar in large bowl; mix well. Add steak. Marinate in refrigerator for 4 to 24 hours. Spoon into cast-iron skillet. Broil until steak is tender and begins to brown. Serve over rice. Yield: 6 servings.

Nancy Billings, Whitesburg Middle School

Teresa's Slow-Cooker Chili

2 to 3 pounds (907 to 1361 g)
  lean ground beef
2 onions, chopped
1 small bell pepper, chopped
1 teaspoon (1.2 g) extra-spicy
  Mrs. Dash seasoning
1 (46-ounce) (3404-g) can
  tomato juice

2 envelopes mild chili seasoning
1 (16-ounce) (454-g) can kidney
  beans, drained
1 (16-ounce) (454-g) can
  tomatoes with green chiles
Salt and pepper to taste
Parsley flakes to taste

Brown ground beef with onions and bell pepper in skillet, stirring until ground beef is crumbly; drain. Combine with remaining ingredients in slow cooker. Cook on High for 1 to 2 hours or until heated through. Yield: 8 to 10 servings.

Tammy Elliott, Nashville Junior High School, Nashville, AR

Chicken Divan

1 (16-ounce) (454-g) package
  frozen broccoli, cooked,
  drained
1 frying chicken, boiled, deboned
2 (10-ounce) (284-g) cans cream
  of chicken soup
1 cup (221 g) mayonnaise

1/4 teaspoon (.5 g) curry powder
1 tablespoon (15 g) lemon juice
1 cup (113 g) shredded Cheddar
  cheese
Buttered bread crumbs or
  crushed chips

Place broccoli in 9x13-inch (23x33-cm) baking dish. Top with chicken. Mix soup, mayonnaise, curry powder and lemon juice in bowl. Pour over chicken. Sprinkle with cheese. Top with bread crumbs. Bake at 400° F (204° C) for 30 minutes or until browned and bubbly. Yield: 6 to 8 servings.

Evelynn Dyer, De Soto High School, De Soto, TX

Springrolls

Using Lumpia (Philippine-style) wrappers will produce a thin and crispy roll, but they require much patience to use. Use supermarket egg roll wrappers if you are short on patience.

3 to 5 tablespoons (41 to 68 g) peanut or corn oil
8 ounces (227 g) ground pork
1 small piece of fresh ginger, minced
1 clove of fresh garlic, minced
1 scallion, minced
4 cups (280 g) thinly shredded Napa cabbage
1 carrot, finely shredded
2 ounces (57 g) cellophane noodles, soaked, cut into 1/2-inch (1.5-cm) lengths
4 dried black Chinese mushrooms

1 tablespoon (18 g) black soy sauce
1 tablespoon (15 g) dry sherry
1 tablespoon (15 g) rice wine vinegar
1 tablespoon (16 g) oyster sauce
2 teaspoons (9.1 g) dark-colored sesame oil
3 tablespoons (24 g) cornstarch
3 tablespoons (44 g) cold water
1 package Lumpia wrappers
2 eggs, lightly beaten
6 to 8 cups (1296 to 1728 g) peanut oil

Heat a wok or large heavy skillet until hot. Add 1 to 2 tablespoons (14 to 27 g) peanut oil, swirling to coat wok. Add pork. Stir-fry until cooked through, breaking into bits. Remove pork from pan and drain. Rinse hot wok with hot water; dry with paper towel. Heat wok again. Add 2 to 3 tablespoons (27 to 41 g) oil, heating until hot but not smoking. Add ginger, garlic, and scallion. Stir-fry for 30 seconds. Toss in cabbage and carrot. Stir-fry for 1 to 2 minutes or until vegetable colors brighten. Add noodles, mushrooms, pork, soy sauce, sherry, vinegar, oyster sauce and sesame oil. Bring to a boil. Mix cornstarch with cold water in bowl. Stir a small amount of mixture into wok. Cook until thickened, stirring frequently and adding more cornstarch mixture if needed. Remove to a plate to cool. Separate wrappers. Brush edges with eggs. Place 2 heaping tablespoons (66 g) pork mixture in shape of cigar 1/3 up from edge of nearest wrapper. Fold bottom of wrapper up and over filling, brushing new surface with eggs. Fold sides over to form 2 straight edges; roll up to enclose. Place seam side down on baking sheet and cover while preparing other rolls. Fill wok, large saucepan or electric deep fryer 1/2 full with remaining peanut oil. Fry 4 or 5 rolls at a time for 2 to 3 minutes or until browned. Remove to baking sheet thickly lined with paper towels to drain. Yield: 12 servings.

Sharen Hanson and Amanda Grue, Manhattan High School, Manhattan, MT

Potato and Sausage Pie

2 cups (600 g) **grated potatoes**
1 tablespoon (10 g) **grated onion**
2 tablespoons (30 g) **water**
1 egg
1 teaspoon (5.5 g) **salt**
¹/₄ teaspoon (.5 g) **pepper**
¹/₄ cup (61 g) **milk**
1 cup (113 g) **shredded Cheddar cheese**

¹/₂ cup (38 g) **sliced tiny smoked sausages**
1 unbaked pie shell
¹/₄ cup (28 g) **shredded Cheddar cheese**
6 to 8 whole tiny smoked sausages

Combine potatoes, onion and water in saucepan. Cook until tender; set aside. Beat egg in bowl. Stir in salt, pepper and milk. Add potato mixture, 1 cup (113 g) cheese and sausage slices; mix well. Spoon into pie shell. Sprinkle with ¹/₄ cup (28 g) cheese. Arrange whole sausages in star shape in center of pie. Bake at 350° F (177° C) for 30 minutes. Yield: 8 servings.

Jane Acevedo, Starr-Iva Middle School, Starr, SC

Uncle Rick's Spaghetti

The name for this came from my sons—we'd have this when Uncle Rick came to visit.

¹/₂ pound (227 g) **bacon, crisp-fried, crumbled**
1 (32-ounce) (907-g) **jar spaghetti sauce**
2 large onions, chopped
1 teaspoon (2.8 g) **minced garlic**
¹/₂ teaspoon (.6 g) **rosemary**

16 ounces (454 g) **Cheddar cheese, shredded**
32 ounces (907 g) **thin spaghetti, cooked**
1 cup (100 g) **grated Parmesan cheese**

Combine bacon, spaghetti sauce, onions, garlic, rosemary and Cheddar cheese in bowl. Add spaghetti and toss to mix. Spoon into 12x18-inch (30x45-cm) baking pan. Top with Parmesan cheese. Bake at 350° F (177° C) for 45 minutes or until bubbly and browned. Serve with garlic bread and salad. Yield: 10 servings.

Sabina L. Pennabaker, Bermudian Springs High School, York Springs, PA

Stromboli

1½ pounds (680 g) **ground beef**
2 loaves **frozen bread dough,**
 thawed
3 tablespoons (47 g) **prepared**
 mustard
12 slices **American cheese**
12 slices **pepperoni or salami**

½ pound (227 g) **thinly sliced**
 cooked ham
4 cups (452 g) **shredded**
 mozzarella cheese
Vegetable oil
Oregano to taste

Brown ground beef in skillet; drain. Roll 1 thawed loaf into 10x16-inch (25x40-cm) rectangle. Spread half of rectangle with half the mustard. Top the mustard layer with half the American cheese, pepperoni, ground beef, ham and mozzarella cheese. Fold plain half of dough over filling, sealing ends well. Brush with oil; sprinkle with oregano. Repeat process with other loaf. Place in 12x18-inch (30x45-cm) baking pans. Bake at 400° F (204° C) for 25 to 30 minutes or until lightly browned. Cool slightly. Cut into 1-inch (2.5-cm) slices. Yield: 16 servings.

Sharlene Book, Oxford High School, Oxford, KS

Arroz con Pollo

1 (2½- to 3-pound) (1134- to
 1361-g) **broiler-fryer, cut up**
1 clove of garlic, sliced
½ teaspoon (2.8 g) **salt**
3 cups (711 g) **water**
1 cup (185 g) **rice**

2 tablespoons (27 g) **vegetable oil**
1 envelope **dip chili mix**
¼ teaspoon (.5 g) **pepper**
2 medium tomatoes, coarsely
 chopped
3 green onions with tops, sliced

Simmer chicken, garlic and salt in water in large saucepan for 30 minutes. Remove chicken; drain, reserving 2 cups (488 g) stock. Let chicken cool. Remove skin and bones; cut into bite-size pieces. Cook rice in oil in skillet over low heat until golden brown, stirring occasionally. Stir in reserved stock, chicken, party dip chili mix and pepper. Bring to a boil; reduce heat. Cover and simmer for 15 minutes. Stir in tomatoes and green onions. Cook, covered, for 5 minutes or until most of liquid is absorbed. Yield: 6 servings.

Chinese Sundaes

1 chicken
2 quarts (2 liters) water
1 cup (160 g) chopped onion
1 cup (120 g) chopped celery
2 teaspoons (11 g) salt
2 teaspoons (3 g) basil

½ teaspoon (1.1 g) pepper
⅓ cup (43 g) cornstarch
1 cup (237 g) water
3 cups (555 g) uncooked rice
   cooked in 6 cups (1422 g)
   water

Combine chicken, 2 quarts (1896 g) water, onion, celery, salt, basil and pepper in large pot. Cook for 30 minutes or until chicken is tender. Remove chicken, reserving stock. Debone and chop cooled chicken. Thicken chicken stock with mixture of cornstarch and 1 cup (237g) water. Add chicken. Serve over rice. Have each guest add favorite toppings selected from bowls of pineapple; chopped apples or peaches; coconut; chopped nuts, green peppers and green onions; grated carrots, cheese and jicama; raisins; and Chinese noodles. Yield: 10 to 12 servings.

Carole Call, Costa Mesa High School, Costa Mesa, CA

Chili Breakfast Burritos

Best served for breakfast, but great anytime.

1 large green bell pepper,
   chopped
⅔ cup (107 g) chopped onion
2 tablespoons (28 g) butter
1 envelope party dip chili mix
8 eggs, lightly beaten

1 cup (113 g) shredded
   Monterey Jack or Cheddar
   cheese
8 (7- to 8-inch) (18- to 20-cm)
   flour tortillas
Sour cream

Cook green pepper and onion in butter in skillet until tender. Add party dip chili mix to eggs in bowl. Scramble well. Stir in cheese; add to skillet. Cook over medium heat until eggs set and cheese melts, stirring often. Remove from heat. Spoon ½ cup (93 g) egg mixture onto each tortilla. Heat tortillas on grill or microwave for 15 seconds each. Spread sour cream over top of each tortilla. Fold to form burritos. Yield: 6 to 8 servings.

Creme de Creme Eggs

2 tablespoons (28 g) **margarine**
6 **eggs, beaten**
2 tablespoons (20 g) **party dip chili mix**

⅓ cup (81 g) **milk**
3 ounces (85 g) **cream cheese, cubed**
Salt to taste

Melt margarine in skillet over low heat. Add mixture of eggs, party dip chili mix and milk. Cook until eggs begin to set, stirring constantly. Add cream cheese and salt. Cook until cream cheese is melted and eggs are cooked, stirring occasionally. Serve with toast and sprinkle with paprika. Yield: 6 servings.

Wild West Omelet

1 tablespoon (14 g) **butter or margarine**
2 **eggs**
1 tablespoon (10 g) **party dip chili mix**

1 tablespoon (15 g) **milk**
¼ cup (28 g) **shredded Cheddar or Monterey Jack cheese**
1 to 2 tablespoons (10 to 20 g) **sliced cooked mushrooms**

Melt butter in omelet pan or skillet over medium-high heat, tilting skillet to coat sides. Beat eggs, party dip chili mix and milk with fork just until whites and yolks are blended. Pour into omelet pan. Cook until set but moist on top. Sprinkle with cheese and mushrooms. Fold in half. Slide onto serving plate. Yield: 1 serving.

A Party Hint

For a Christmas family brunch, serve "make-your-own waffles." Have several family members bring their waffle irons so that three or four are baking at the same time. Serve a variety of fruit toppings on buttermilk, whole wheat and chocolate chip waffles.

Denver Dipper San

2 tablespoons (13 g) chopped
  green bell pepper
2 tablespoons (20 g) chopped
  onion
2 tablespoons (28 g) margarine
1 tablespoon (10 g) party dip
  chili mix

6 eggs, beaten
1/2 cup (70 g) chopped ham
1/4 cup (61 g) milk
8 ounces (227 g) cream cheese,
  cubed
3 English muffins, split, toasted

Sauté green pepper and onion in margarine in skillet. Combine party dip chili mix, eggs, ham and milk in bowl. Add to skillet. Cook over low heat until eggs begin to set, stirring occasionally. Add cream cheese. Cook until cream cheese is melted and eggs are cooked, stirring occasionally. Cover each muffin half with egg mixture. Yield: 3 to 6 servings.

Turkey Chili San

8 ounces (227 g) cream cheese,
  cubed
1 cup (244 g) milk
1/2 cup (50 g) grated Parmesan
  cheese

1 tablespoon (10 g) party dip
  chili mix
6 white bread slices, toasted
6 slices hot cooked turkey

Heat cream cheese and milk in saucepan over low heat; stir until smooth. Stir in Parmesan cheese and party dip chili mix. Cover each toast slice with turkey and cream cheese sauce. Yield: 6 servings.

A Party Hint

For outdoor parties, serve finger foods or fork foods in individual baskets. Each guest will have a small basket filled with the entire meal—foods such as chicken nuggets, deviled eggs, biscuits, fruit kabobs, and desserts, such as brownies. The baskets can be colorful or natural with the only color being the napkin liner.

Doodles of Noodles

½ cup (80 g) **chopped onion**
1 tablespoon (14 g) **margarine**
8 ounces (227 g) **cream cheese,**
   cubed
½ cup (115 g) **sour cream**
2 tablespoons (20 g) **party dip**
   chili mix

½ cup (122 g) **milk**
1 (10-ounce) (284-g) **package**
   frozen peas, cooked, drained
1 teaspoon (5.1 g) **lemon juice**
½ teaspoon (2.8 g) **salt**
4 ounces (113 g) **noodles,**
   cooked, drained

Sauté onion in margarine in skillet. Add cream cheese, sour cream, party dip chili mix and milk. Cook over low heat until cream cheese is melted, stirring frequently. Add peas, lemon juice and salt; mix well. Combine cream cheese mixture and hot noodles; mix lightly. Yield: 4 to 6 servings.

Burro Russo

½ cup (114 g) **melted butter**
¼ cup (66 g) **tomato paste**
½ cup (121 g) **half-and-half**
½ teaspoon (.3 g) **crumbled sage**
1½ teaspoons (3.5 g) **Hungarian**
   sweet paprika

Salt to taste
2 to 4 cloves of garlic, minced
¾ cup (75 g) **(or more)**
   Parmesan cheese

Whisk butter into mixture of tomato paste and half-and-half in saucepan. Add seasonings and garlic; mix well. Simmer for 2 to 3 minutes. Whisk in Parmesan cheese. Serve over hot pasta. Yield: 4 servings.

Julia White, Jarrell High School, Jarrell, TX

A Party Hint

Give an engagement shower where everyone fills a brown paper bag with food that starts with the gift-giver's first or last name. Have the engaged couple look through the bag's contents and guess who gave them the food. This is a wonderful way to fill the couple's kitchen.

Pasta with Garlic, Broccoli and Sun-Dried Tomatoes

Florets of 1 bunch broccoli
16 ounces (454 g) rotini pasta
1/4 cup (54 g) olive oil
12 cloves of garlic, chopped
1/2 cup (54 g) chopped sun-dried
   tomatoes, drained
2 large tomatoes, seeded,
   chopped

1/2 teaspoon (.4 g) dried red
   pepper
1 cup (100 g) grated Parmesan
   cheese
1 tablespoon (4.5 g) dried basil
Grated Parmesan cheese to taste

Cook broccoli in water to cover in large pot just until tender. Remove to colander with slotted spoon, reserving cooking liquid. Cook pasta in reserved cooking liquid just until tender; drain. Heat oil in skillet over medium heat. Add garlic. Sauté for 2 minutes. Add tomatoes, red pepper and broccoli. Sauté until heated through. Add pasta, 1 cup (100 g) cheese and basil; toss until well blended. Sprinkle with cheese. Yield: 6 servings.

Parrie Kay Newman, Cedar Hill High School, Cedar Hill, TX

Shrimp Pasta

1 or 2 medium onions, cut into
   thin wedges
2 cloves of garlic, minced
2 tablespoons (27 g) olive oil
1 pound (454 g) medium shrimp,
   peeled, deveined
2 medium green bell peppers,
   cut into short thin strips

1 envelope party dip chili mix
1 (28-ounce) (794-g) can whole
   tomatoes, drained, chopped
1/2 cup (21 g) shredded fresh basil
1/2 teaspoon (.4 g) oregano
   leaves, crushed
8 ounces (227 g) hot cooked
   linguini

Cook onions and garlic in olive oil in large skillet until onions are tender but not brown. Add shrimp and green peppers. Cook for 4 minutes or until shrimp is cooked through, stirring constantly. Add party dip chili mix, tomatoes, basil and oregano; heat through. Toss with linguini. May substitute 1 to 1 1/2 tablespoons (4.5 to 6.8 g) dried basil for the fresh basil. Yield: 6 servings.

Side Dishes

Calico Beans

3 pounds (1361 g) ground beef
Chopped onion to taste
4 slices bacon, crisp-fried,
  crumbled
1 (16-ounce) (454-g) can lima
  beans, drained
1 (16-ounce) (454-g) can butter
  beans, drained
1 (16-ounce) (454-g) can kidney
  beans, drained
1 (16-ounce) (454-g) can
  ranchero beans

1 (16-ounce) (454-g) can pinto
  beans with jalapeño
1 (16-ounce) (454-g) can pork
  and beans
1/4 cup (61 g) catsup
1 teaspoon (5.5 g) salt
1/8 teaspoon (.3 g) pepper
1 tablespoon (16 g) prepared
  mustard
2 tablespoons (30 g) vinegar
1/2 cup (91 g) packed brown
  sugar

Brown ground beef in skillet, stirring until crumbly; drain. Stir in onion, bacon and beans. Mix remaining ingredients in bowl. Stir into bean mixture. Spoon into slow cookier. Cook on High for 2 hours. Yield: 10 to 12 servings.

Chris Ellingson, McClintock High School, Tempe, AZ

Marinated Carrots

1 onion, thinly sliced
1 green bell pepper, sliced
2 pounds (907 g) tiny whole
  carrots, cooked
1 (10-ounce) (284-g) can tomato
  soup
³/₄ cup (180 g) vinegar
¹/₄ cup (55 g) vegetable oil

1 cup (200 g) sugar
1 tablespoon (16 g) prepared
  mustard
1 tablespoon (17 g)
  Worcestershire sauce
1 tablespoon (17 g) salt
¹/₈ to ¹/₄ teaspoon (.3 to .5 g)
  pepper

Combine onion, green pepper and carrots in large bowl; mix well. Combine remaining ingredients in saucepan; mix well. Cook until heated through. Pour over carrot mixture. Chill, covered, overnight. Keeps well in refrigerator for several days. Yield: 8 to 10 servings.

Melanie Bratcher, Bert Rumble Middle School, Warner Robins, GA

Greek Potatoes

5 large baking potatoes
2 lemons
2 teaspoons (12 g) garlic salt

¹/₂ cup (108 g) olive oil
1 tablespoon (2.3 g) whole
  oregano

Wash potatoes. Cut each into 8 long strips; do not peel. Place in shallow baking pan. Squeeze lemons over potatoes. Sprinkle with garlic salt. Pour oil over potatoes. Sprinkle with oregano. Bake at 350° F (177° C) for 40 minutes. Serve hot. Yield: 10 servings.

Brenda L. Little, D.H. Conley High School, Greenville, NC

A Party Hint

Have your next Fourth of July barbecue outdoors with a patriotic red, white and blue theme—checkered blankets, fireworks and flags for decoration. Serve fruit salad, barbecued chicken, baked beans, cold salads, hamburgers, hot dogs, chips, cold beer or soda, homemade lemonade, iced tea and various pies.

Party Potatoes

1 cup (237 g) water
1/2 cup (80 g) chopped onion
1/2 (10-ounce) (284-g) can reduced-fat and reduced-sodium cream of chicken soup
1/2 cup (126 g) evaporated milk
1/4 teaspoon (.5 g) pepper
1 cup (113 g) shredded reduced-fat Cheddar cheese

1 cup (227 g) nonfat sour cream
1 (32-ounce) (907-g) package frozen loose-pack hashed brown potatoes
2 cups (150 g) crushed cornflakes
1 tablespoon (14 g) melted margarine

Bring water and onion to a boil in saucepan; reduce heat. Simmer, covered, for 2 to 4 minutes. Remove from heat; do not drain. Combine with soup, evaporated milk and pepper in bowl; mix well. Stir in cheese, sour cream and potatoes. Spoon into 9x13-inch (23x33-cm) baking dish sprayed with nonstick cooking spray. Bake, covered, at 350° F (177° C) for 1 hour. Remove cover and stir. Toss cornflakes with margarine in bowl. Sprinkle over potato mixture. Bake, uncovered, for 30 to 40 minutes longer. Yield: 8 servings.

Deb McKay, Grafton Junior High School, Grafton, ND

Great Potato Bake

2 slices bacon, chopped
1/2 cup (80 g) chopped onion
1/2 cup (50 g) chopped green bell pepper
8 ounces (227 g) cream cheese, cubed

1 cup (244 g) milk
2 tablespoons (20 g) party dip chili mix
4 cups (488 g) thinly sliced potatoes

Fry bacon in skillet until crisp; remove from skillet. Drain, reserving 1 tablespoon (14 g) drippings. Sauté onion and green pepper in reserved pan drippings. Add cream cheese, milk and party dip chili mix. Cook over low heat until cream cheese is melted, stirring frequently. Add potatoes; mix lightly. Spoon into 6x10-inch (15x25-cm) baking dish; sprinkle with bacon. Bake at 350° F (177° C) for 50 to 55 minutes or until potatoes are tender. Yield: 6 servings.

Sweet Potato Casserole

3 cups (600 g) stewed sweet
  potatoes, mashed
1 cup (200 g) sugar
1/3 cup (81 g) milk
1/2 cup (114 g) butter
1 teaspoon (4.8 g) vanilla extract

1 cup (181 g) packed light brown
  sugar
1/2 cup (63 g) flour
1/3 cup (76 g) butter, softened
1 cup (119 g) chopped pecans

Combine sweet potatoes, sugar, milk, 1/2 cup (114 g) butter and vanilla in bowl; mix well. Spoon into 9x9-inch (23x23-cm) baking dish. Mix brown sugar, flour, 1/3 cup (76 g) butter and pecans in bowl. Sprinkle over casserole. Bake at 350° F (177° C) for 25 minutes. Yield: 6 to 8 servings.

Judy Daves, Trumann High School, Trumann, AR

Veggie Mix Fix

8 ounces (227 g) cream cheese,
  cubed
1/2 cup (122 g) milk
1 (10-ounce) (284-g) package
  frozen mixed vegetables,
  cooked, drained

1/4 teaspoon (1.4 g) salt
Dash of pepper
2 tablespoons (20 g) party dip
  chili mix
1 cup (210 g) mashed potatoes
1 small tomato, sliced

Heat cream cheese and milk in saucepan over low heat; stir until smooth. Add mixed vegetables and seasonings; mix well. Pour into 1-quart (1-liter) casserole. Cover with mashed potatoes; top with tomato slices. Bake at 350° F (177° C) for 20 minutes. Yield: 8 servings.

A Party Hint

Decorate your windows for Christmas with ornaments cut with holiday cookie cutters. This adds a holiday touch to your windows and a wonderful aroma to the house. These can also be added to holiday greenery arrangements for tables.

Chili Chives Sauce

8 ounces (227 g) **cream cheese,**
  cubed
¹/₂ cup (122 g) **milk**
1 tablespoon (10 g) **party dip**
  chili mix

1 tablespoon (3 g) **chopped**
  chives
1 teaspoon (5.1 g) **lemon juice**
¹/₄ teaspoon (1.5 g) **garlic salt**

Heat cream cheese and milk in saucepan over low heat until smooth, stirring constantly. Stir in remaining ingredients. Serve over hot cooked potatoes, green beans, broccoli or asparagus. Yield: 6 to 8 servings.

Spice-of-Life Sauce

8 ounces (227 g) **cream cheese,**
  cubed
¹/₄ cup (61 g) **milk**
¹/₂ teaspoon (2.8 g)
  Worcestershire sauce

1 tablespoon (10 g) **party dip**
  chili mix
¹/₄ teaspoon (1.3 g) **prepared**
  horseradish
Salt to taste

Heat cream cheese and milk in saucepan over low heat until smooth, stirring constantly. Stir in remaining ingredients. Chill. Serve over shrimp, cold vegetables or hard-cooked eggs. Yield: 6 to 8 servings.

A Party Hint

For a south-of-the-border fiesta, send invitations on red chile designs reading "some like it hot." Decorate with hanging red chiles or ristras intermingled with lights shaped like red chiles.

Finishing Touches

Cakes and Cookies

Best One-Bowl Chocolate Cake

1³/₄ cups (191 g) **cake flour, sifted**
1¹/₂ cups (300 g) **sugar**
1 teaspoon (3 g) **baking powder**
¹/₂ teaspoon (2.8 g) **salt**
¹/₂ teaspoon (1.5 g) **baking soda**
5 tablespoons (27 g) **baking cocoa**

¹/₂ cup (103 g) **shortening**
1 tablespoon (14 g) **butter, softened**
1 cup (244 g) **milk**
2 **eggs**
1 teaspoon (4.8 g) **vanilla extract**

Sift flour, sugar, baking powder, salt, baking soda and baking cocoa into large mixer bowl. Add shortening, butter and ²/₃ cup (163 g) of the milk. Mix at low speed for 1 minute. Beat for 1¹/₂ minutes. Add remaining ¹/₃ cup (81 g) milk, eggs and vanilla. Beat for 2 minutes. Pour into 2 greased and floured 8-inch (20-cm) round cake pans. Bake at 350° F (177° C) for 30 minutes or until edges pull away from pans; do not overbake. Cool in pans for 5 minutes. Remove to wire rack to cool completely. Frost cake as desired
Yield: 12 to 16 servings.

Jeanette O. Cook, West Monroe High School, West Monroe, LA

Cheese Chess Cake

1 package yellow cake mix
1 egg
1/2 cup (114 g) melted margarine
2 eggs

1 (1-pound) (454-g) package
confectioners' sugar
8 ounces (227 g) cream cheese,
softened

Combine cake mix, 1 egg and margarine in bowl; mix well. Press into greased 9x13-inch (23x33-cm) baking pan. Mix remaining ingredients in bowl. Pour over top. Bake at 325° F (163° C) for 45 minutes. Yield: 12 to 15 servings.

Debra C. Lane, Princeton School, Princeton, NC

Decadent Fudge Cake

1 cup (227 g) butter or
margarine, softened
1 1/2 cups (300 g) sugar
4 eggs
2 1/2 cups (313 g) flour
1/2 teaspoon (1.5 g) baking soda
1 cup (245 g) buttermilk
2 (4-ounce) (113-g) bars sweet
baking chocolate, melted,
cooled

1 cup (170 g) semisweet
chocolate chips
1/3 cup (100 g) chocolate syrup
2 teaspoons (9.6 g) vanilla extract
4 ounces (113 g) chopped white
chocolate
2 tablespoons (26 g) shortening
1/2 cup (85 g) semisweet
chocolate chips
2 teaspoons (8.5 g) shortening

Cream butter and sugar in mixer bowl at medium speed. Beat in eggs 1 at a time. Add flour to creamed mixture alternately with mixture of next 2 ingredients, beginning and ending with flour. Stir in melted chocolate, 1 cup (170 g) chocolate chips, syrup and vanilla until blended. Spoon into greased and floured 10-inch (25-cm) bundt pan. Bake at 300° F (149° C) for 1 hour and 25 minutes or until cake springs back when lightly touched. Invert onto serving plate. Combine white chocolate and 2 tablespoons (26 g) shortening in double boiler. Bring water to a boil; reduce heat to low. Cook until mixture is melted and smooth, stirring frequently; remove from heat. Drizzle over cooled cake. Melt 1/2 cup (85 g) chocolate chips and 2 teaspoons (8.5 g) shortening in saucepan over low heat, stirring frequently. Cool. Drizzle over white chocolate. Garnish with chocolate leaves. Yield: 16 servings.

Janice Lee, Rockdale ISO, Rockdale, TX

Nutty Pumpkin Crumble

2½ cups (615 g) canned
  pumpkin
1 (12-ounce) (340-g) can
  evaporated skim milk
2 eggs
½ cup (100 g) sugar or 12
  envelopes Equal

1 teaspoon (2.3 g) cinnamon
½ teaspoon (1.2 g) nutmeg
½ teaspoon (1.1 g) cloves
½ teaspoon (.9 g) ginger
1 package yellow cake mix
½ cup (114 g) melted margarine
1 cup (119 g) chopped pecans

Combine pumpkin, evaporated milk, eggs, sugar and spices in bowl; mix well. Pour into nonstick 9x13-inch (23x33-cm) cake pan. Sprinkle dry cake mix over pumpkin mixture. Drizzle with margarine. Sprinkle with pecans. Bake at 350° F (177° C) for 50 minutes or until golden brown. Chill overnight. Garnish with light whipped topping. Yield: 16 servings.

Nancy Karnes, Hopewell Junior School, West Chester, OH

Punch Bowl Cake

1 package yellow cake mix
2 packages banana pudding mix
4 cups (976 g) milk
1 (16-ounce) (454-g) jar
  strawberry fruitspread

1 (16-ounce) (454-g) can crushed
  pineapple, drained
16 ounces (454 g) whipped
  topping

Prepare and bake cake mix using package directions for 9x13-inch (23x33-cm) cake pan. Break cooled cake into pieces. Prepare pudding using package directions with 4 cups (976 g) milk. Alternate layers of cake, fruitspread, pineapple, pudding and whipped topping in glass punch bowl until all ingredients are used, ending with whipped topping. Chill for 2 hours. Yield: 12 servings.

Judy S. Ferrell, Columbus High School, Columbus, GA

A Party Hint

When decorating a cake for your next party, dip knife in water then spread frosting. The frosting will spread much smoother.

Sour Cream Coffee Cake

3 cups (375 g) **flour**
1¹/₂ teaspoons (4.5 g) **baking powder**
1¹/₂ teaspoons (4.5 g) **baking soda**
¹/₂ teaspoon (2.8 g) **salt**
³/₄ cup (170 g) **butter**
1¹/₂ cups (300 g) **sugar**
3 **eggs**
2 teaspoons (9.6 g) **vanilla extract**
2 cups (460 g) **sour cream**

³/₄ cup (136 g) **packed brown sugar**
2 teaspoons (4.5 g) **cinnamon**
1 cup (119 g) **coarsely chopped pecans**
1¹/₂ cups (180 g) **confectioners' sugar**
2 tablespoons (30 g) **water**
¹/₂ teaspoon (2.4 g) **vanilla extract**

Sift first 4 ingredients together. Cream butter and sugar in mixer bowl until light and fluffy. Add eggs 1 at a time, beating well after each addition. Stir in 2 teaspoons (9.6 g) vanilla. Add flour mixture and sour cream alternately to creamed mixture, beating well after each addition. Mix brown sugar, cinnamon and pecans in small bowl. Spoon ¹/₃ of the batter into greased and floured 10-inch (25-cm) tube or bundt pan. Sprinkle with ¹/₃ of the pecan mixture. Repeat layers twice. Bake at 350° F (177° C) for 1 hour or until coffee cake tests done. Cool in pan for 5 minutes. Invert onto serving plate. Combine confectioners' sugar, water and ¹/₂ teaspoon (2.4 g) vanilla in bowl; mix until of glaze consistency. Drizzle over cake. Yield: 16 servings.

Fern D. Wilson, North Adams Jr. High School, Seaman, OH

Super Cookie

¹/₂ cup (114 g) **butter, softened**
¹/₃ cup (60 g) **packed brown sugar**
¹/₄ cup (50 g) **sugar**
1 **egg**

1¹/₃ cups (167 g) **flour**
¹/₂ teaspoon (1.5 g) **baking soda**
¹/₄ teaspoon (1.4 g) **salt**
¹/₄ teaspoon (1.2 g) **vanilla extract**
¹/₂ cup (85 g) **chocolate chips**

Cream butter, brown sugar and sugar in mixer bowl until light. Beat in egg. Add flour, baking soda and salt; mix well. Stir in vanilla. Fold in chocolate chips. Spread evenly with damp hand on greased pizza pan. Bake at 350° F (177° C) for 15 to 20 minutes or until light brown. Yield: 8 to 10 servings.

Pat Burkholder, Carroll County High School, Hillsville, VA

Chocolate Banana Brownies

1¼ cups (156 g) **flour**
1 teaspoon (5.5 g) **salt**
½ teaspoon (1.5 g) **baking powder**
½ teaspoon (1.1 g) **cinnamon**
¼ teaspoon (.8 g) **baking soda**
1 cup (170 g) **semisweet chocolate chips**

¼ cup (57 g) **butter or margarine**
½ cup (100 g) **sugar**
¼ cup (57 g) **butter or margarine, softened**
1 **egg**
¼ cup (61 g) **milk**
1½ cups (338 g) **mashed bananas**
½ cup (60 g) **chopped pecans**

Sift flour, salt, baking powder, cinnamon and baking soda together. Melt chocolate chips and ¼ cup (57 g) butter in saucepan, stirring to blend. Let stand to cool. Cream sugar and ¼ cup (57 g) butter in mixer bowl until light and fluffy. Beat in egg, milk and bananas. Add flour mixture gradually, beating well after each addition. Divide batter into 2 equal portions. Stir pecans and chocolate mixture into 1 portion. Layer half the chocolate batter, all the plain batter and remaining chocolate batter in greased and floured 9x9-inch (23x23-cm) baking pan. Marbleize batter with knife. Bake at 350° F (177° C) for 25 to 30 minutes or until done. Cool in pan. Cut into 3-inch (7.5-cm) squares. Yield: 6 to 8 servings.

Kristi Wakefield, Buffalo High School, Buffalo, TX

Grandma's Cookies

3¼ cups (406 g) **flour, sifted**
1 teaspoon (3 g) **baking powder**
1 teaspoon (3 g) **baking soda**
½ teaspoon (1.1 g) **cinnamon**
¾ teaspoon (1.7 g) **cloves**
½ teaspoon (.9 g) **ginger**
1 teaspoon (5.5 g) **salt**

2 cups (363 g) **packed dark brown sugar**
1 cup (205 g) **shortening**
2 **eggs**
1 cup (240 g) **cold coffee**
1 teaspoon (4.8 g) **vanilla extract**
1½ cups (248 g) **seedless raisins**

Sift first 7 ingredients together. Cream brown sugar with shortening in mixer bowl. Mix in eggs and coffee. Add flour mixture gradually, beating well after each addition. Stir in vanilla and raisins. Drop by teaspoonfuls onto greased cookie sheet. Bake at 375° F (191° C) for 12 minutes. Cool on wire rack. Yield: 48 servings.

Diane Johnson, Carney High School, Carney, OK

Monster Cookies

1 cup (181 g) **packed brown sugar**
1 cup (200 g) **sugar**
¹/₂ cup (114 g) **margarine, softened**
3 eggs
1 teaspoon (4.8 g) **vanilla extract**
1 teaspoon (6.8 g) **light corn syrup**

1¹/₂ cups (384 g) **peanut butter**
2 teaspoons (6 g) **baking soda**
4¹/₂ cups (365 g) **rolled oats**
1 cup (170 g) **semisweet chocolate chips**
4 ounces (113 g) **"M & M's" Plain Chocolate Candies**

Combine all ingredients in bowl in order listed; mix well. Drop by teaspoonfuls onto ungreased cookie sheet. Bake at 350° F (177° C) for 10 minutes. Yield: 84 servings.

Parrie Kay Newman, Cedar Hill High School, Cedar Hill, TX

Paintbrush Cookies

Be an artist and design your own cookie shapes. Almost every children's story includes an animal, fruit or character that could be used for a storybook cookie.

1 cup (205 g) **shortening**
1 cup (120 g) **confectioners' sugar, sifted**
1 egg
1¹/₂ teaspoons (7.2 g) **almond extract**

1 teaspoon (4.8 g) **vanilla extract**
2¹/₂ cups (288 g) **sifted flour**
1 teaspoon (3 g) **baking powder**
1 teaspoon (5.5 g) **salt**
2 egg yolks
Food coloring

Mix shortening and confectioners' sugar in bowl. Stir in egg and flavorings. Add flour, baking powder and salt; mix well. Roll ¹/₄ inch (.75 cm) thick on lightly floured board. Cut into different shapes with cookie cutters dipped in flour. Place on cookie sheet. Beat egg yolks with fork in bowl. Place equal portions in several small custard cups. Add desired food coloring to each cup. Thin with drops of water if needed. Use small clean paintbrushes to paint designs on cookies. Bake at 350° F (177° C) for 8 to 10 minutes. Colors will be clearer if cookies do not brown. Yield: 24 servings.

LaDell Emmons, McAlester High School, McAlester, OK

Boiled Peanut Butter Oatmeal Cookies

2 cups (400 g) sugar
1/2 cup (122 g) milk
1/2 cup (114 g) margarine
1 tablespoon (21 g) corn syrup

1/2 cup (128 g) peanut butter
2 1/2 cups (203 g) oats
1/4 cup (30 g) chopped pecans

Bring sugar, milk, margarine and corn syrup to a boil in double boiler over hot water. Simmer for 2 minutes; remove from heat. Stir in peanut butter, oats and pecans quickly. Drop by spoonfuls onto greased waxed paper. Let stand to cool and harden. Yield: 24 servings.

Teena Ruth, Provine High School, Jackson, MS

Cheesecake Bars

2/3 cup (80 g) finely crushed
  graham crackers
1/2 cup (63 g) flour
1/2 cup (60 g) chopped pecans
1/4 cup (50 g) sugar
1/2 cup (114 g) melted butter or
  margarine
1/3 cup (67 g) sugar

8 ounces (227 g) cream cheese,
  softened
1 egg
1/2 teaspoon (1 g) grated lemon
  rind
1 tablespoon (15 g) lemon juice
2 tablespoons (15 g) finely
  crushed graham crackers

Mix 2/3 cup (80 g) crumbs, flour, pecans and 1/4 cup (50 g) sugar in bowl. Stir in butter until crumbly. Pat into ungreased 9x9-inch (23x23-cm) baking pan. Bake at 350° F (177° C) for 12 minutes. Cream 1/3 cup (67 g) sugar with cream cheese in mixer bowl until light and fluffy. Beat in egg, lemon rind and lemon juice. Pour over baked layer. Bake at 350° F (177° C) for 20 to 25 minutes. Sprinkle with remaining 2 tablespoons (15 g) crumbs. Cool completely. Cut into bars. Store in refrigerator. Yield: 36 servings.

Kacie Campbell and Jenny Joffman, Walnut High School, Walnut, IA

Glowing Jack-O-Lanterns

2 cups (250 g) **flour**
1¹/₂ teaspoons (4.5 g) **baking powder**
¹/₄ teaspoon (1.4 g) **salt**
6 tablespoons (85 g) **butter or margarine, softened**
¹/₃ cup (68 g) **shortening**

³/₄ cup (150 g) **sugar**
1 egg
1 tablespoon (15 g) **milk**
1 teaspoon (4.8 g) **vanilla extract**
3 ounces (85 g) **sour hard candy, crushed**

Sift flour, baking powder and salt together. Beat butter with shortening in mixer bowl for 30 seconds. Add sugar; beat until light and fluffy. Beat in egg, milk and vanilla. Add flour mixture gradually, beating well after each addition. Chill, covered, for 3 hours. Divide dough into halves. Chill 1 half. Roll other half ¹/₄ inch (.75 cm) thick on lightly floured surface. Cut into 4- to 5-inch (10- to 13-cm) circles. Place 2 inches (5 cm) apart on foil-lined baking sheet. Repeat with remaining dough. Cut eyes, nose and mouth from each circle with sharp knife. Fill holes with crushed candy. Bake at 375° F (191° C) for 8 to 10 minutes or until edges are lightly browned. Cool on baking sheet for 10 minutes. Remove to wire racks to cool completely.
Yield: 24 to 36 servings.

Kacie Campbell and Jenny Joffman, Walnut High School, Walnut, IA

A Party Hint

Set up a water park party for preschoolers—several sprinklers (different types), two or three baby pools, a "slip and slide" or other water games. For party favors give out sunglasses or plastic visors with names painted on them. Play water balloon toss. Serve cake with blue (water) frosting with a brown sugar edge (sandy beach). With frosting tips make starfish and sea creatures. Cover a cupcake completely with frosting and shape to resemble a whale. Be sure to have plenty of adults to supervise every pool area.

Desserts

Banana Cream Pie

3 cups (732 g) **milk**
4¹/₂ **tablespoons** (35 g) (heaping) **flour**
1¹/₂ **tablespoons** (12 g) (heaping) **cornstarch**
³/₄ **cup** (150 g) **sugar**
¹/₄ **teaspoon** (1.4 g) **salt**

2 **eggs, slightly beaten**
1 **teaspoon** (4.8 g) **vanilla extract**
2 to 4 **bananas, sliced**
1 **baked (9-inch)** (23-cm) **pie shell**
8 **ounces** (227 g) **whipped topping**

Scald milk in top of double boiler. Combine flour, cornstarch, sugar and salt in bowl; mix well. Add to scalded milk. Cook for 15 minutes, stirring constantly. Stir a small amount of hot mixture into beaten eggs; stir eggs into hot mixture. Cook for several minutes longer. Cool. Stir in vanilla. Layer pudding and bananas ¹/₂ at a time in pie shell. Spread whipped topping over pie. Chill in refrigerator. Yield: 6 to 8 servings.

Shirley Stewart, Albany High School, Albany, MT

Banana Salad Dessert

1 cup (221 g) **mayonnaise**
¹/₄ cup (61 g) **milk**
6 **underripe bananas, cut into**
  2-inch (5-cm) **pieces**

3 cups (225 g) **ground Spanish**
  peanuts

Mix mayonnaise and milk in bowl. Roll banana pieces through mayonnaise mixture to coat. Roll through peanuts. Yield: 18 servings.

Helen Lewis, Starspencer High School, Spencer, OK

Classic Boston Cream Pie

1¹/₄ cups (156 g) **flour**
1¹/₂ teaspoons (4.5 g) **baking**
  powder
¹/₄ teaspoon (1.4 g) **salt**
¹/₃ cup (68 g) **shortening**
1 cup (200 g) **sugar**
2 **eggs**
1 teaspoon (4.8 g) **vanilla extract**
³/₄ cup (183 g) **milk**
¹/₃ cup (67 g) **sugar**

2 tablespoons (16 g) **cornstarch**
1³/₄ cups (427 g) **milk**
2 **egg yolks, slightly beaten**
1 tablespoon (14 g) **butter**
1 teaspoon (4.8 g) **vanilla extract**
3 tablespoons (44 g) **water**
2 tablespoons (28 g) **butter**
3 tablespoons (16 g) **baking cocoa**
1 cup (120 g) **confectioners' sugar**
¹/₂ teaspoon (2.4 g) **vanilla extract**

Sift first 3 ingredients together. Cream shortening, 1 cup (200 g) sugar, eggs, and 1 teaspoon (4.8 g) vanilla in mixer bowl until light. Add flour mixture and ³/₄ cup (183 g) milk alternately to creamed mixture, beating well after each addition. Pour into greased and floured 9-inch (23-cm) round cake pan. Bake at 350° F (177° C) for 30 minutes or until cake tests done. Cool in pan for 10 minutes. Remove to wire rack to cool completely. Cut horizontally into 2 layers. Bring ¹/₃ cup (67 g) sugar, cornstarch, 1³/₄ cups (183 g) milk and egg yolks to a boil in saucepan, stirring constantly. Simmer for 1 minute, stirring constantly; remove from heat. Beat in 1 tablespoon (14 g) butter and 1 teaspoon (4.8 g) vanilla. Chill, covered. Spread between cake layers. Bring water and 2 tablespoons (28 g) butter to a boil in saucepan; remove from heat. Stir in cocoa quickly. Beat in confectioners' sugar and ¹/₂ teaspoon (2.4 g) vanilla until smooth. Cool. Drizzle over cake. Yield: 10 servings.

Carole C. DeArman, Berkner High School, Richardson, TX

Low-Fat Cherry Delight

2 teaspoons (5 g) **sugar-free lemon gelatin**
1/3 cup (79 g) **boiling water**
8 ounces (227 g) **low-fat cream cheese, softened**

1/2 cup (33 g) **light whipped topping**
1 **graham cracker pie shell**
1 (20-ounce) (567-g) **can light cherry pie topping**

Dissolve gelatin in boiling water. Whip cream cheese in mixer bowl. Beat in gelatin mixture. Fold in whipped topping. Spoon into pie shell. Chill for several hours. Spread pie with topping or spoon 1/4 cup (17 g) topping over each slice. Yield: 8 servings.

Judy Geurin, Harmony Grove High School, Benton, AR

Butterfinger Ice Cream

2 cups (400 g) **sugar**
4 **eggs, beaten**
1 cup (256 g) **crunchy peanut butter**
3 quarts (3 liters) **milk**
1 **can sweetened condensed milk**

1 **can evaporated milk**
2 tablespoons (29 g) **vanilla extract**
1/8 teaspoon (.7 g) **salt**
6 **large Butterfinger candy bars, frozen, crushed in packages**

Add sugar to beaten eggs in bowl gradually, mixing well after each addition. Add peanut butter and milks gradually, mixing well after each addition. Beat in flavoring, salt and candy. Pour into 6-quart (6-liter) ice cream freezer container. Freeze using manufacturer's directions. Yield: 24 to 30 servings.

Donna Anderson, Kelly R-IV School, Benton, MO

A Party Hint

Give each shower guest a specific time of day for which their gift should be used (such as 7:30 pm to 9:00 pm). The gift would then be one for preparing or eating dessert, for example.

Pavlova

Pavlova normally consists of a meringue topped with whipped cream and berries or other fruit. It is a dessert of Australian origin and is very popular for special celebrations.

6 egg whites, at room
  temperature
$^1/_4$ teaspoon (1.4 g) salt
$1^1/_2$ teaspoons (5 g) cream of
  tartar
$1^1/_2$ cups (300 g) sugar

1 teaspoon (4.8 g) vanilla extract
Frozen fat-free vanilla yogurt,
  softened
1 quart (664 g) strawberries,
  sliced

Beat egg whites in mixer bowl until frothy. Sprinkle salt and cream of tartar over top. Beat until stiff but not dry. Beat in sugar gradually. Beat in vanilla until mixture is stiff. Spread $^1/_3$ of meringue to within 1 inch (2.5 cm) of edge of 12-inch (30-cm) chop plate. Pile remaining meringue around meringue base to a height of approximately $2^1/_2$ inches (6.5 cm), leaving center unfilled. Bake at 250° F (121° C) for $1^1/_4$ hours. Turn off oven. Let stand in oven for 15 minutes longer. Cool completely. Fill center with yogurt. Top with mounds of strawberries. Yield: 8 to 12 servings.

Kevin Nelson, Bloomingdale High School, Bloomingdale, MN

Strawberry Pizza

$1^1/_2$ cups (188 g) flour
$^1/_4$ cup (45 g) packed brown sugar
1 cup (227 g) melted margarine
1 cup (119 g) chopped pecans
2 cups (240 g) confectioners'
  sugar

8 ounces (227 g) cream cheese,
  softened
16 ounces (454 g) whipped
  topping
1 can strawberry pie filling

Sift flour into bowl. Stir in brown sugar and margarine. Add pecans; mix well. Press into 9x13-inch (23x33-cm) baking pan. Bake at 400° F (204° C) for 12 minutes. Cool in pan. Cream confectioners' sugar with cream cheese in mixer bowl until light and fluffy. Fold in whipped topping. Spread over cooled crust. Top with pie filling. Chill until serving time. Yield: 15 servings.

Kay Mardis, Arab High School, Arab, AL

Mini Strawberry Pizzas

1 package strawberry gelatin pie
  filling
2¼ cups (281 g) **flour**
2 teaspoons (6 g) **baking powder**
½ teaspoon (2.8 g) **salt**
½ cup (114 g) **butter or**
  margarine, softened
1 cup (200 g) **sugar**

1 **egg**
¼ cup (61 g) **milk**
½ teaspoon (2.4 g) **vanilla extract**
8 ounces (227 g) **cream cheese,**
  softened
½ cup (100 g) **sugar**
1 quart (576 g) **strawberries**

Prepare pie filling using package directions. Sift flour, baking powder and salt together. Cream butter and 1 cup (200 g) sugar in mixer bowl until light. Add egg, milk and vanilla; beat well. Add sifted mixture; mix well. Chill thoroughly. Shape into cookies. Place on baking sheet. Bake at 375° F (191° C) for 7 to 8 minutes or until golden brown. Cool completely. Mix cream cheese with ½ cup (100 g) sugar in bowl. Spread over cookies. Top with pie filling and strawberries. May use other fruits for different look. Yield: 36 servings.

Jane Martin Acevedo, Starr-Iva Middle School, Starr, SC

Fruit Pizza Tart

1 cup (227 g) **unsalted cream**
  butter, softened
½ cup (100 g) **sugar**
2½ cups (313 g) **flour**
⅓ cup (81 g) **milk**
9 ounces (255 g) **cream cheese,**
  softened

¾ cup (90 g) **confectioners' sugar**
1 teaspoon (2 g) **grated orange**
  rind
1 tablespoon (16 g) **orange juice**
1 pint (332 g) **strawberries, sliced**
1 pint (290 g) **blueberries**
¼ cup (72 g) **melted apple jelly**

Cream butter and sugar in mixer bowl until light and fluffy. Add flour and milk; beat at low speed until well mixed. Press onto bottom and ½ inch (1.5 cm) up sides of 9x13-inch (23x33-cm) baking pan. Prick bottom with fork. Bake at 400° F (204° C) for 15 to 18 minutes or until lightly browned. Combine next 4 ingredients in mixer bowl. Beat at medium speed until light and fluffy. Spread over cooled crust. Chill for 1 hour or until firm. Arrange fruit over filling. Brush fruit with melted jelly. Yield: 18 servings.

Carolyn B. Swanson, Northern Vance High School, Henderson, NC

Fruited Trifle

You may substitute any vanilla pudding instead of making your own; you may use angel food cake instead of pound cake; and you may use whipped topping instead of whipping the cream yourself. This dessert is prettiest when served in a trifle dish and garnished. My students love it!

3/4 cup (150 g) sugar
1/3 cup (42 g) flour or 3
　tablespoons (24 g) cornstarch
1/4 teaspoon (1.4 g) salt
2 cups (488 g) milk
3 egg yolks, slightly beaten
2 tablespoons (28 g) butter
1 teaspoon (4.8 g) vanilla extract
1 (16-ounce) (454-g) pound cake,
　cut into 1/2-inch (1.5-cm) slices

1/4 to 1/2 cup (62 to 124 g) fruit
　juice
1 pint (332 g) strawberries, sliced
2 bananas, peeled, sliced
1 (11-ounce) (312-g) can
　mandarin orange sections
4 kiwifruit, peeled, sliced
1 cup (238 g) whipping cream
2 tablespoons (15 g)
　confectioners' sugar

Combine sugar, flour and salt in saucepan. Stir in milk gradually. Cook over medium heat until bubbly, stirring constantly. Cook for 2 minutes longer, stirring constantly; remove from heat. Stir a small amount of hot mixture into egg yolks; stir egg yolks into hot mixture. Cook for 2 minutes, stirring constantly; remove from heat. Beat in butter and vanilla. Chill pudding until set. Brush cake slices generously with fruit juice. Arrange half the slices in single layer in trifle or other deep bowl. Layer with half the strawberries, bananas, orange sections and kiwifruit. Spoon half the pudding over fruit. Repeat layers with remaining cake, fruit and pudding. Whip cream in bowl until soft peaks form. Add confectioners' sugar gradually, beating constantly until stiff peaks form. Spoon or pipe over top of trifle. Garnish with whole strawberries and mint sprigs. Chill until serving time. Yield: 20 servings.

Ann Anderson, Duncanville High School, Duncanville, TX

A Party Hint

Have a Christmas party tradition that is different from the usual "eat, sit around and chat" parties. Invite several couples to play "reindeer games." Serve the fairly usual party food but instead of chit-chat, everyone wears reindeer antlers (party favors which were given out at the door) and plays a variety of games (board games or adult trivia-type games).

Rhubarb Crisp

3 to 4 cups (366 to 488 g)
  chopped rhubarb
1½ cups (300 g) **sugar**
½ cup (91 g) **packed brown sugar**
2 tablespoons (16 g) **cornstarch**

½ cup (114 g) **butter**
¾ cup (136 g) **packed brown sugar**
¾ cup (61 g) **rolled oats**
¾ cup (94 g) **flour**

Mix rhubarb, sugar, ½ cup (91 g) brown sugar and cornstarch in bowl. Spoon into 9x9-inch (23x23-cm) baking dish. Cut butter into ¾ cup (136 g) brown sugar in bowl. Stir in oats and flour. Sprinkle over rhubarb mixture. Bake at 375° F (191° C) for 30 to 35 minutes or until rhubarb is tender.
Yield: 6 to 8 servings.

Alta Faye Simmons, Pershing Middle School, Springfield, MO

Dirt Cups

2 cups (488 g) **cold milk**
1 (4-ounce) (113-g) **package**
  chocolate instant pudding mix
8 ounces (227 g) **whipped topping**

1 (16-ounce) (454-g) **package chocolate sandwich cookies, crushed**

Pour milk into large bowl. Add pudding mix. Beat with wire whisk for 1 to 2 minutes or until well blended. Let stand for 5 minutes. Stir in whipped topping and half the cookie crumbs. Place 1 tablespoon (13 g) crushed cookies into each of eight to ten 7-ounce (198-g) plastic cups. Fill ¾ full with pudding mixture. Top with remaining cookie crumbs. Chill for 1 hour. Decorate with gummy worms and frogs, candy flowers or chopped peanuts.
Yield: 8 to 10 servings.

Mary K. Warren, Blacksburg High School, Blacksburg, VA

A Party Hint

Have an end of the school year celebration with the theme "come play in the dirt again." Centerpieces can be of butternut squash with onion flowers. The main attraction can be a mud pie served from a flowerpot with a spade.

Cookie Cake

1 (16-ounce) (454-g) package
    Oreo cookies
1/4 cup (57 g) melted margarine
1 (4-ounce) (113-g) package
    chocolate instant pudding mix
2 cups (488 g) milk

8 ounces (227 g) **cream cheese,**
    softened
1/4 cup (30 g) **confectioners' sugar**
12 ounces (340 g) **whipped**
    topping

Crush cookies, reserving 3/4 cup (90 g) crumbs. Mix remaining crumbs with margarine in bowl. Press into 9x13-inch (23x33-cm) dish. Mix pudding mix with milk using package directions. Chill until set. Mix cream cheese, confectioners' sugar and 1/3 of the whipped topping in bowl. Spread cream cheese mixture over cookie crumb layer. Spread pudding over cream cheese mixture. Top with remaining whipped topping. Sprinkle with reserved crumbs. Chill until serving time. Cut into squares. Yield: 15 servings.

Mickey G. Weikle, Pulaski Middle School, Pulaski, VA
Beverley C. Cole, Chilhowie High School, Chilhowie, VA

Oreo Dessert

1 large package Oreo cookies
1/2 gallon (1056 g) **vanilla ice**
    cream, softened
2 bottles of chocolate magic
    shell syrup

16 ounces (454 g) **whipped**
    topping
Chopped pecans or walnuts
Maraschino cherries

Crumble cookies into 10x15-inch (25x37.5-cm) pan. Spread ice cream over crumbs. Drizzle syrup over ice cream. Spread with whipped topping. Top with pecans and cherries. Freeze until firm. Let stand for 30 to 45 minutes to come to room temperature before serving. Yield: 12 to 15 servings.

Sharon Stewart, Avery County High School, Newland, NC

Chocolate Frozen Dessert

1 cup (125 g) flour
1 cup (119 g) chopped pecans
1/2 cup (114 g) melted margarine
1/4 cup (20 g) rolled oats
1/4 cup (45 g) packed brown sugar

1 (12-ounce) (340-g) jar
  butterscotch topping
1/2 gallon (1056 g) chocolate ice
  cream, softened

Mix flour, pecans, margarine, oats and brown sugar in bowl. Press into 9x13-inch (23x33-cm) baking pan. Bake at 350° F (177° C) for 10 minutes or until lightly browned. Watch carefully; this burns easily. Let stand to cool. Crumble mixture; remove 1/2 of the crumbs for topping. Drizzle half the butterscotch topping over crumbs in pan. Top with ice cream. Drizzle remaining butterscotch topping over ice cream. Sprinkle with reserved crumbs. Freeze until serving time. Yield: 15 servings.

Colleen Liebhart, Kirksville High School, Kirksville, MO

Eclair Dessert

You may substitute light pudding, skim milk and light whipped topping to reduce fat in this recipe.

1 (16-ounce) (454-g) package
  graham crackers
2 (4-ounce) (113-g) packages
  vanilla instant pudding mix
3 cups (732 g) milk
8 ounces (227 g) whipped
  topping

1 cup (200 g) sugar
1/2 cup (114 g) butter or
  margarine
1/3 cup (81 g) milk
1/2 cup (85 g) semisweet
  chocolate chips
1/2 cup (60 g) chopped pecans

Layer 1/3 of the graham crackers in 9x13-inch (23x33-cm) dish. Beat pudding mix with milk at low speed in mixer bowl for 2 minutes or until blended. Fold in whipped topping. Spoon half the mixture over graham crackers in dish. Repeat layers; top with remaining graham crackers. Bring sugar, butter and milk to a boil in saucepan. Simmer for 1 minute, stirring frequently; remove from heat. Stir in chocolate chips. Spoon over layers. Top with pecans. Chill, covered, for 8 hours. Yield: 12 to 15 servings.

Karen Smith, Northside High School, Warner Robins, GA

Frozen Treats

1 (4-ounce) (113-g) package
  vanilla instant pudding mix
1 cup (244 g) milk
8 ounces (227 g) whipped
  topping

1 cup (225 g) mashed bananas
1 pint (288 g) strawberries,
  mashed

Prepared pudding using package directions and 1 cup (244 g) milk. Fold in whipped topping and fruit. Spoon into paper drinking cups. Insert wooden sticks. Freeze until firm. Peel off paper. Yield: 6 to 8 servings.

Judy Meek, Wilbur Middle School, Wichita, KS

Four-Layer Dessert

You may wish to use different flavors of pudding mix in this dessert, such as chocolate and butter pecan.

1 cup (125 g) flour
1/2 cup (114 g) margarine
1 cup (119 g) chopped pecans
8 ounces (227 g) cream cheese,
  softened
1 cup (75 g) whipped topping

1 cup (120 g) confectioners'
  sugar
3 (2-ounce) (58-g) packages
  instant pudding mix
3 cups (732 g) milk
Whipped topping

Mix flour, margarine and pecans in bowl. Press into 9x13-inch (23x33-cm) baking pan. Bake at 350° F (177° C) for 20 minutes. Blend cream cheese, 1 cup (75 g) whipped topping and confectioners' sugar in bowl. Spread over slightly cooled crust. Mix pudding mix with milk. Spread over cream cheese layer. Alternate rows of pudding if using 2 flavors. Spread with additional whipped topping. Garnish with chopped nuts, semisweet chocolate chips, cherries, coconut or other favorites. Yield: 18 to 24 servings.

Donna J. Shaw, 8th and Lincoln, Galena, KS

Kahlúa Carmelo Sauce

3 cups (138 g) miniature
  marshmallows
1¼ cups (227 g) packed light
  brown sugar

1 cup (238 g) whipping cream
¼ cup (57 g) Kahlúa
¼ cup (57 g) butter
1½ teaspoons (7.2 g) vanilla

Bring marshmallows, brown sugar, whipping cream and Kahlúa to a boil in heavy saucepan, stirring until sugar is dissolved. Cook to 224° F (107° C) degrees on candy thermometer, stirring occasionally; remove from heat. Add butter and vanilla. Cool. Serve warm or at room temperature on ice cream or in parfaits. Store in refrigerator. Yield: 2¼ cups (723 g).

Margaret Miller, Eldridge High School, Virginia Beach, VA

Melba Sauce

1 (10-ounce) (284-g) package
  frozen raspberries, thawed
½ cup (144 g) red currant jelly
¼ cup (50 g) sugar

1 tablespoon (15 g) lemon juice
¼ teaspoon (.5 g) grated lemon
  rind
Dash of salt

Simmer raspberries in covered saucepan for 15 minutes. Press through fine strainer into 1-cup (250 ml) measure. Add enough water to measure ⅔ cup (158 g). Combine with remaining ingredients in saucepan. Simmer until smooth, stirring constantly. Store in airtight container in refrigerator. Serve with strawberries and whipped cream for a delicious dessert.
Yield: 1¼ cups (651 g).

Nancy Deeds, Harvell High School, Manilla, Iowa

A Party Hint

For a pre-game meal, decorate the table with plates and napkins reflecting school colors. Place balloons around the room. Serve food suitable for athletes.

Mississippi Mud Sauce

Serve this sauce over ice cream or pound cake for a super-rich, super-quick dessert.

³/₄ cup (150 g) **sugar**
¹/₃ cup (29 g) **baking cocoa**
1 (5-ounce) (142-g) **can evaporated milk**

¹/₄ cup (64 g) **peanut butter**

Combine sugar, baking cocoa and evaporated milk in saucepan. Bring to a boil over medium-high heat, stirring constantly; remove from heat. Stir in peanut butter. Serve warm. Yield: 1¹/₂ cups (384 g).

Kathy Peery, Graham Middle School, Bluefield, VA

Puppy Chow

1 (1-pound) (454-g) **package confectioners' sugar**
¹/₂ cup (114 g) **margarine**

1 cup (256 g) **peanut butter**
2 cups (340 g) **chocolate chips**
1 small package Crispix cereal

Empty confectioners' sugar into large non-recycled brown paper bag. Combine margarine, peanut butter and chocolate chips in saucepan. Cook until melted, stirring frequently. Pour quickly over cereal in bowl, mixing lightly. Pour into prepared paper bag and shake well. Spoon into party bowl. Yield: 50 servings.

M.C. Potter, Bay High School, Bay, AR

A Party Hint

For great gifts or to give your home a holiday aroma, tie 1 stick cinnamon, broken, ¹/₂ teaspoon (1 g) whole allspice, 1¹/₂ teaspoons (6.6 g) whole cloves, three (¹/₂x¹/₂-inch) (1.5x1.5-cm) pieces gingerroot in cheesecloth or decorative material. Simmer in desired liquid in saucepan.

Old McDonald Days

Barbecued Chicken — Slaw — Dips

Fresh Vegetables — Corn on the Cob
(*All home-grown if possible!*)

Southern Sweet Tea and Lemonade

Apple Pies — Freshly Churned Ice Cream

Provide a few bales of hay for seating; a few tailgates to put plates and cups on; rocking chairs and a hammock under the trees for reclining; and, fresh flowers, including Queen Anne's lace from the roadside. Use plenty of denim, bright colors, old plates and cups. To complete the event, have wagon rides following the meal.

A Party Hint

Use a "Country Christmas" theme for ease and economy in serving a crowd during the holidays. Use an antique quilt or comforter, or holiday print cloth for a table cover. For table decorations, use a favorite holiday item or collection or mix santas, small trees and candles (use antique bobbins with brass and/or copper candle sticks) of various heights and diameters. Be sure to highlight decorative items—especially framed prints or needlework with the candlelight. Combine antique boxes, baskets, and bowls (with a colored cloth napkin as a liner) with wood and crockery pieces for serving utensils. Serve punch from a stone jar or iced drinks in stone jars. Plan cookies that may be stacked in baskets, a cake that can be served from a plate (not individual pieces), cheese spreads instead of cheese balls, etc.

Substitutions

	Instead of	Use
Baking	1 teaspoon baking powder	1/4 teaspoon baking soda plus 1/2 teaspoon cream of tartar
	1 tablespoon cornstarch (for thickening)	2 tablespoons all-purpose flour or 1 tablespoon tapioca
	1 cup sifted all-purpose flour	1 cup plus 2 tablespoons sifted cake flour
	1 cup sifted cake flour	1 cup minus 2 tablespoons sifted all-purpose flour
	1 cup dry bread crumbs	3/4 cup cracker crumbs
Dairy	1 cup buttermilk	1 cup sour milk or 1 cup yogurt
	1 cup heavy cream	3/4 cup skim milk plus 1/3 cup butter
	1 cup light cream	7/8 cup skim milk plus 3 tablespoons butter
	1 cup sour cream	7/8 cup sour milk plus 3 tablespoons butter
	1 cup sour milk	1 cup milk plus 1 tablespoon vinegar or lemon juice or 1 cup buttermilk
Seasoning	1 teaspoon allspice	1/2 teaspoon cinnamon plus 1/8 teaspoon cloves
	1 cup catsup	1 cup tomato sauce plus 1/2 cup sugar plus 2 tablespoons vinegar
	1 clove of garlic	1/8 teaspoon garlic powder or 1/8 teaspoon instant minced garlic or 3/4 teaspoon garlic salt or 5 drops of liquid garlic
	1 teaspoon Italian spice	1/4 teaspoon each oregano, basil, thyme, rosemary, plus dash of cayenne pepper
	1 teaspoon lemon juice	1/2 teaspoon vinegar
	1 tablespoon mustard	1 teaspoon dry mustard
	1 medium onion	1 tablespoon dried minced onion or 1 teaspoon onion powder
Sweet	1 1-ounce square chocolate	1/4 cup baking cocoa plus 1 teaspoon shortening
	1 2/3 ounces semisweet chocolate	1 ounce unsweetened chocolate plus 4 teaspoons granulated sugar
	1 cup honey	1 to 1 1/4 cups sugar plus 1/4 cup liquid or 1 cup corn syrup or molasses
	1 cup granulated sugar	1 cup packed brown sugar or 1 cup corn syrup, molasses or honey minus 1/4 cup liquid

Metric Equivalents

Although the United States has opted to postpone converting to metric measurements, most other countries, including England and Canada, use the metric system. The following chart provides convenient approximate equivalents for allowing the use of regular kitchen measures when cooking from foreign recipes.

Volume

These metric measures are approximate benchmarks
for purposes of home food preparation.
1 milliliter = 1 cubic centimeter = 1 gram

Liquid	Dry
1 teaspoon = 5 milliliters	1 quart = 1 liter
1 tablespoon = 15 milliliters	1 ounce = 30 grams
1 fluid ounce = 30 milliliters	1 pound = 450 grams
1 cup = 250 milliliters	

Weight	Length
1 ounce = 28 grams	1 inch = 2$\frac{1}{2}$ centimeters
1 pound = 450 grams	$\frac{1}{16}$ inch = 1 millimeter

Formulas Using Conversion Factors

When approximate conversions are not accurate enough,
use these formulas to convert measures from one system to another.

Measurements	Formulas
ounces to grams:	# ounces x 28.3 = # grams
grams to ounces:	# grams x 0.035 = # ounces
pounds to grams:	# pounds x 453.6 = # grams
pounds to kilograms:	# pounds x 0.45 = # kilograms
ounces to milliliters:	# ounces x 30 = # milliliters
cups to liters:	# cups x 0.24 = # liters
inches to centimeters:	# inches x 2.54 = # centimeters
centimeters to inches:	# centimeters x 0.39 = # inches

Approximate Weight to Volume

Some ingredients which we commonly measure by volume are measured by weight in foreign recipes. Here are a few examples for easy reference.

flour, all-purpose, unsifted	1 pound = 450 grams = 3 1/2 cups
flour, all-purpose, sifted	1 pound = 450 grams = 4 cups
sugar, granulated	1 pound = 450 grams = 2 cups
sugar, brown, packed	1 pound = 450 grams = 2 1/4 cups
sugar, confectioners'	1 pound = 450 grams = 4 cups
sugar, confectioners', sifted	1 pound = 450 grams = 4 1/2 cups
butter	1 pound = 450 grams = 2 cups

Temperature

Remember that foreign recipes frequently express temperatures in Centigrade rather than Fahrenheit.

Temperatures	Fahrenheit	Centigrade
room temperature	68°	20°
water boils	212°	100°
baking temperature	350°	177°
baking temperature	375°	190.5°
baking temperature	400°	204.4°
baking temperature	425°	218.3°
baking temperature	450°	232°

Use the following formulas when temperature conversions are necessary.

Centigrade degrees x $9/5$ + 32 = Fahrenheit degrees
Fahrenheit degrees - 32 x $5/9$ = Centigrade degrees

American Measurement Equivalents

1 tablespoon = 3 teaspoons	12 tablespoons = 3/4 cup
2 tablespoons = 1 ounce	16 tablespoons = 1 cup
4 tablespoons = 1/4 cup	1 cup = 8 ounces
5 tablespoons + 1 teaspoons = 1/3 cup	2 cups = 1 pint
8 tablespoons = 1/2 cup	4 cups = 1 quart
	4 quarts = 1 gallon

Index

**GREAT AMERICAN
OPPORTUNITIES**